Nikolai Gumilev
ON
RUSSIAN
POETRY

Edited & translated by David Lapeza

Ardis   Ann Arbor

CONTENTS

Illustrations − frontispiece

Top − Gumilev with son and wife (Anna Akhmatova)
Bottom left − Gumilev
Bottom right − Gumilev at Guild of Poets

ON RUSSIAN POETRY

THE LIFE OF VERSE

I

The peasant plows, the stonemason builds, the priest prays and the judge judges. What does the poet do? Why doesn't he expound in easily memorized verses on the sprouting conditions of various grasses, why does he refuse to compose a new "Dubinushka" or sweeten the bitter medicine of religious theses? Why only in moments of faint-heartedness will he admit that he aroused good feelings with his lyre? Is there really no place for the poet in society, no matter whether among the bourgeois, the social democrats or in the religious community? Let John the Damascene[1] be silent!

This is what the champions of the thesis of "Art for life" say. Hence—François Coppée, Sully Prudhomme, Nekrasov[2] and, in many ways, Andrei Bely.

The defenders of "Art for art" retort: "Go away, what does the peaceful poet have to do with you.... You offend his soul, like coffins, even now you have whips, dungeons, axes for your stupidity, enough of you, mad slaves.... For us, princes of Song, sovereigns of castles of dream, life is merely a means of flight: the harder a dancer strikes the earth with his feet the higher he soars. Whether we chase our verses like goblets, or write obscure, nearly drunken ditties, we are always, and above all, free, and scarcely wish to be useful."

Hence—Hérédia, Verlaine, and in our country, Maikov.

This controversy will continue many centuries more without leading to any results, and that is not surprising, for in any attitude toward anything, whether toward people, things or ideas, we require first of all that it be chaste. By this I mean the right of every phenomenon to be valuable in itself, not to require justification of its existence, and another, higher right to serve others.

Homer sharpened his hexameters, unconcerned with anything except vowel and consonant sounds, caesurae and spondees, and adapted his content to them. However, he would have considered himself a bad craftsman if, hearing his songs, youths had not striven for martial glory, if the clouded gaze of maidens had not increased the beauty of peace.

There is an unchasteness of attitude in both the doctrine of

11

"Art for life," and that of "Art for art."

In the first case, art is reduced to the level of a prostitute or a soldier. Its existence has value only to the extent that it serves goals extraneous to it. It would not be surprising if the eyes of the gentle muses were to grow dull, and they were to develop bad manners.

In the second case, art becomes effete, grows agonizingly moonlike; Mallarmé's words, put in the mouth of his Herodiade,[3] are applicable to it:

> I love the horror of being virgin and I want
> to live amidst the terror my hair inspires....

Purity is suppressed sensuality, and it is beautiful; the absence of sensuality is frightening, like a new unheard-of form of depravity.

No! cries the era of esthetic puritanism, of great demands on the poet as creator, on idea or word as artistic material. The poet must place upon himself the fetters of difficult forms (recall Homer's hexameters, Dante's terze rime and sonnets, the Old Scottish stanzas of Byron's poems) or ordinary forms, but in their development carried to the point of impossibility (Pushkin's iambs), he must, but only in praise of his God, whom he is obliged to have. Otherwise he would be a simple gymnast.

Still, if I were to choose between the two above doctrines, I would say that in the first there is greater respect for art and understanding of its essence. There is a new aim imposed upon it, a new application is indicated for the powers seething within it, even if it is an unworthy base application—that is not important: isn't the cleaning of the Augean stables referred to on an equal basis with the other great feats of Hercules? In ancient ballads it is told that Roland was depressed when a dozen enemies rode out against him. He could fight beautifully and worthily only against hundreds. However, one should not forget that even Roland could be defeated....

Now I shall speak only of poetry, recalling Oscar Wilde's words, which horrified the weak and inspired courage in the strong:

> For the material that the painter or sculptor uses is meager in comparison with that of words. Words have not merely music as sweet as

12

that of viol and lute, color as rich and vivid as any that makes lovely for us the canvas of the Venetian or the Spaniard, and plastic form no less sure and certain than that which reveals itself in marble or in bronze, but thought and passion and spirituality are theirs also, are theirs, indeed, alone."[4]

And that verse is the highest form of speech, everyone knows who, carefully sharpening a piece of prose, used force to restrain the arising rhythm.

II

The origin of individual poems is mysteriously similar to the origin of living organisms. The poet's thought receives a shock from the external world, sometimes in an unforgettably clear moment, sometimes dimly, like conception in sleep, and for a long time it is necessary to bear the foetus of the future creation, heedin the timid movements of the still weak new life. Everything affects the course of its development—a beam of the horned moon, an unexpectedly heard melody, a book read, a flower's smell. Everything determines its future fate. The ancients respected the silent poet, as one respects a woman preparing to be a mother.

Finally, in the labor, like the labor of childbirth (Turgenev speaks of this), the poem appears. It is lucky if, in the moment of its appearance, the poet is not distracted by some considerations extraneous to art, if, gentle as a dove, he strives to convey what was born at full term, finished, and tries, wise as a serpent, to include all this in the most perfect form.

Such a poem can live for centuries, moving from temporary oblivion to new glory, and even dead, will, like King Solomon, long inspire in men a sacred trembling. Such is the *Iliad*....

But there are poems not born at full term, in which, around the original impressions, others did not manage to accumulate, and there are those in which, on the contrary, details obscure the basic theme; they are cripples in the world of images, and the perfection of their separate parts does not gladden, but rather saddens us, like the beautiful eyes of hunchbacks. We are much obliged to hunchbacks, they tell us surprising things, but sometimes you dream with such longing of the svelte youths of Sparta, that you no longer pity their weak brothers and sisters, condemned by a stern law. This is what Apollo wants, a rather frightening, cruel, but terribly beautiful god.

What is necessary for a poem to live, and not in a jar of alcohol, like some curious freak, not the half-life of the invalid in a wheelchair, but a full and powerful life—for it to arouse love and hatred, to make the world reckon with the fact of its existence? What requirements must it satisfy?

I would answer in short: *all.*

Really, it must have: thought and feeling—without the first, the most lyrical poem will be dead, and without the second, even an epic ballad will appear a dull contrivance (Pushkin in his lyrics and Schiller in his ballads knew this), —the softness of outline of a young body, where nothing stands out, nothing is wasted, and the definition of a statue in sunlight; simplicity—only for it is the future open, and—refinement, as a living recognition of the continuity of all joys and sorrows of past ages; and above all that—style and gesture.

In style God emerges from his creation, the poet gives himself away, this secret self, unknown even to him, and allows us to guess the color of his eyes, the shape of his hands. And that is so important. For we love Dante Alighieri, the boy in love with Beatrice's pale face, the frenzied Ghibelline and the Veronese exile, no less than his *Divine Comedy*.... By gesture in a poem I mean such an arrangement of words, choice of vowel and consonant sounds, acceleration and deceleration of rhythm that the reader of the poem strikes the pose of its hero, copies his facial expressions and movements and, thanks to the suggestion of his own body, experiences what the poet himself did, so that the spoken idea becomes no longer a lie, but the truth. Poets' complaints about the fact that the public, intoxicated with the music of verse, does not sympathize with their sufferings, are based on misunderstanding. The joy, the sorrow, the despair the reader feels are only *his own.* To arouse sympathy, one must speak of oneself in a clumsy manner, as Nadson did.[6]

I return to the preceding: to be worthy of its name, a poem, having the qualities enumerated, must preserve complete harmony among them and, what is most important, be called to life not "by irritation of a captive thought," but by internal necessity, which gives it a living soul—a temperament. Besides that, it must be irreproachable even in their irregularity. Because, only conscious departures from the generally accepted norms give a poem individuality, though they love to disguise themselves as unconscious ones. Thus, Charles Asselineau[7] tells of an "uncontrolled sonnet," where the author, consciously breaking the rules, pretends that he does it in a burst of poetic inspiration or a fit of passion. Ronsard, Maynard, Malherbe[8] wrote such sonnets. These irregularities play the role of birthmarks, through them it is easiest of all to recall to mind the appearance of the whole.

In short, a poem must be a copy of the beautiful human body, that highest level of perfection imaginable: not without reason did men create even the Lord God in their own image and likeness. Such a poem is valuable in itself, it has the right to exist at all costs. Thus to save one man, expeditions are prepared in which dozens of other men perish. But, yet, once he is saved, he must, as everyone else, justify to himself his own existence.

III

Really, the world of images is closely connected with the world of men, but not as people usually believe. Not being an analogy of life, art does not have an existence completely like ours, cannot convey to us a perceptible link with other realities. Poems written even by true visionaries in moments of trance have meaning only insofar as they are good. To think otherwise is to repeat the famous mistake of the sparrows that wanted to peck painted fruit.

But beautiful poems, like living beings, enter the circle of our life; they now instruct, now appeal, now bless; among them are guardian angels, wise leaders, tempter demons and dear friends. Under their influence men love, hate and die. In many respects they are the highest judges, like the totems of the North American Indians. For example—Turgenev's "Quiet Backwater," where the poem "The Upas-tree," by its strength and remoteness, precipitates the denouement of a solitary love, painful in the Russian fashion;[9] or—Dostoevsky's The Idiot, when "The Poor Knight" resounds like an incantation on the lips of Aglaya, mad with a thirst to love the hero;[10] or—Sologub's "Night Dances" with their poet, captivating willful princesses with the marvelous music of Lermontovian stanzas.[11]

In contemporary Russian poetry, as an example of such "living" poems, I will point out just a few, attempting only to illustrate the above, and setting aside much that is important and characteristic. Here, for example, is a poem by Valery Bryusov, "In the Crypt":

You are laid out in the tomb in myrtle crown.
I kiss the moon's reflection on your face.

Through latticed windows the circle of the moon is seen.
In the clear sky, as above us, the secret of silence.

Behind you at your pillow a wreath of damp roses,
On your eyes, like pearls, drops of former tears.

A moon beam, caressing the roses, silvers the pearls,
Moonlight circles round the ancient marble slabs.

What do you see, what remember in your unwaking sleep?
Dark shadows bend ever lower towards me.

I came to you into the tomb through the black garden.
By the doors lemurs maliciously watch over me.

I know, I know I won't be long alone with you!
The moonlight completes its measured circle path.

You are motionless, you are beautiful, in myrtle crown.
I kiss the light of heaven on your face!

Here, in this poem, the Bryusovian passion, allowing him to treat even the supreme terror of death, of disappearance, thoughtlessly, and the Bryusovian tenderness, a tenderness almost maidenly, which is delighted by everything, tormented by everything, the moonbeams, the pearls, the roses—these two most characteristic qualities of his work help him to create an image, a copy perhaps, of the momentary meeting of lovers irrevocably separated and forever poisoned by this separation.

In the poem "The Heliads"[12] (*Transparence*, p. 124)[13] Vyacheslav Ivanov, the poet, through his sunniness and purely masculine power, so different from the lunar femininity of Bryusov, offers an image of Phaethon. He transforms the bright ancient tale into eternally young truth. There have always been men condemned to perish by the very nature of their daring. But they did not always know that defeat could be more fruitful than victory.

> He was beautiful, proud youth,
> Son of the Sun, young Sun-god,
> When he siezed with firm hand
> The fateful pledge of grandeur—
>
> When from the blushing Horae,
> He carried off the reins of his realm—
> And the steeds struggled against the gates,
> Smelling the flaming expanse!
>
> And, freed, flew up, neighed,
> Deserting the scarlet prison,
> And ran with the clatter of brazen hoofs,
> Obedient to the light yoke . . . etc.

The "proud youth" does not appear in the poem itself, but we see him in the words and songs of the three maiden Heliads, in love with him, pushing him toward his doom and mourning him "on the green Eridanus." And agonizingly enviable is the fate of that one, of whom maidens sing such songs!

Innokenty Annensky is also powerful, but with a power that is not so much Manly as Human. With him feeling does not give birth to thought, as usually happens in poets, rather the thought itself grows so strong that it becomes feeling, alive even to the point of pain. He loves only "today" and only "here," and this love leads him not only to the pursuit of decoration, but of decorativeness. His verses suffer from this, they inflict incurable wounds upon the soul and one must fight against them with the incantations of time and space.

> What grave, dark delirium!
> How turbid, moony these summits!
> To touch violins so many years
> And not recognize their strings in the light!
>
> Who needs us? Who lit

Two yellow, two melancholy faces?
And suddenly felt the bow
That someone took and someone merged them.

Oh, how long ago! Through this darkness
Say one thing: —are you she, she?
And the strings fawned upon him,
Ringing, but, fawning, trembled.

Isn't it so? Never more
Shall we part—all right?
And the violin answered, "Yes,"
But the violin's heart ached.

The bow understood everything, it fell silent,
But in the violin the echo was sustained,
And it was torture for them,
What seemed music to men.

But the man did not put out
The light until morning . . . and the strings sang,
Only morning found them exhausted
On the black velvet of their bed.

To whom has this not happened? Who has not had to bow over their dream, feeling that the possibility of realizing it has been irrevocably lost? And he who, having read this poem, forgets the eternal, virginal freshness of the world, believes that there is only torment, even if it seems like music, he is lost, he is poisoned. But are we not captivated by the thought of death from such a melodious arrow?

Next, passing over Blok's "Lady"—there is so much written about her—I will say something about Kuzmin's *Chimes of Love*.[14] The author simultaneously wrote music to them, and this gave them the mark of a certain special exaltation and elegance, accessible only to pure sounds. The verse flows, like a stream of thick, fragrant and sweet honey, you believe that it alone is the natural form of human speech, and a conversation or prose passage afterwards would seem somehow dreadful, like a whisper in the Tyutchevian night, like an evil spell. This poem is composed of a series of lyrical passages, hymns to love and about love. Its words can be repeated every day, as you repeat a prayer, inhale the scent of perfume, look at flowers. I include one passage from it, which completely captivates our conception of tomorrow, makes it a cornucopia:

> Love sets out nets
> Of strongest silks;
> Lovers, like children,
> Look for chains.
>
> Yesterday, you know not love,
> Today you're all aflame.
> Yesterday you reject me,
> Today vow to me.
>
> Tomorrow the beloved will love
> And the unbeloved yesterday,
> He'll come to you who was not
> Other evenings.
>
> Fall in love, who will fall in love
> When the time comes,
> And what will be, will be,
> What fate prepared for us.
>
> We, like little children,
> Look for chains,
> And blindly fall into the nets
> Of strongest silks.

Thus art, born of life, approaches it again, but not as trifling laborer, not as peevish grumbler, but as equal to equal.

IV

A few days ago the journal *The Scales*, the main bulwark of Russian Symbolism, ceased its existence. Here are several characteristic sentences from the final manifesto of the editorial staff, printed in No. 12:

> *The Scales* has been the floodgate, which was essential until such time as the two ideological levels of the age merged, and it becomes useless when this is achieved, finally, by its own actions. Together with

the victory of the ideas of Symbolism in the form in which *The Scales* professed and had to profess them, the journal itself becomes unnecessary. The aim is achieved and *eo ipso* the means is aimless! There will be other aims!

We do not wish to say by this that the Symbolist movement has died, that Symbolism has ceased to play the role of the watch-word of our age.... But tomorrow the same word will become another watchword, will burn with a different flame, and it already burns in a different way above us.

It is impossible not to agree with all of this, especially if the matter concerns poetry. Russian Symbolism, represented most completely in *The Scales*, irrespective of the fact that it is an inevitable stage in the history of the human spirit, had also an assignment as champion of cultural values, which, from Pisarev to Gorky, have been treated very unceremoniously. It has carried out this assignment brilliantly and inspired the barbarians of the Russian press, if not with respect for great names and ideas, then at least with fear of them. But the question of whether it should exist as a literary school now has too little hope of being completely resolved, because Symbolism was created not by the mighty will of a single person, as Parnasse by the will of Leconte de Lisle, and was not the result of social upheaval, like Romanticism, but was the result of the maturation of the human spirit, which declared the world our own conception. So that it will appear obsolete only when mankind renounces this thesis—and renounces it not only on paper, but with its entire being. When this will happen, I leave for the philosophers to judge. Now we cannot but be Symbolists. This is not an appeal, nor a wish, it merely a fact to which I can attest.

Apollo, 1910, No. 7, pp. 5-14.

ACMEISM AND THE LEGACY OF SYMBOLISM

It is clear to the attentive reader that Symbolism has completed its circle of development and is now declining. There is the fact that Symbolist works hardly ever appear anymore, and if any do appear, then ones that are extremely weak, even from the point of view of Symbolism, and that, more and more frequently voices are raised in favor of a reconsideration of values and reputations indisputable not so long ago, and that the Futurists, the Ego-Futurists, and other hyenas that always follow the lion have appeared.[1] To replace Symbolism there is a new movement, which, whatever it is called—Acmeism (from the word ακμή—the highest degree of something, the flower, the time of flowering), or Adamism (a manfully firm, clear view of life), —demands, in any case, greater balance of powers and a more exact knowledge of the relationships between subject and object than there was in Symbolism. However, for this trend to establish itself fully and be a worthy successor to what preceded it, it must accept the latter's legacy and answer all the questions it posed. The glory of one's forebears carries obligations, and Symbolism was a worthy father.

French Symbolism, the ancestor of all Symbolism as a school, moved purely literary questions into the foreground—free verse, a more original and vacillating style, metaphor elevated above all else, and the notorious "theory of correspondences." This last betrays its non-Romance and consequently non-national, alien basis. The Romance spirit is too beloved of the element of light, which separates objects, draws careful, clear lines; but this Symbolist merging of all images and objects, the changeability of their appearance, could have arisen only in the misty gloom of Germanic forests. A mystic would say that Symbolism in France is a direct result of Sedan.[2] But at the same time it revealed in French literature an aristocratic craving for the unusual and the difficult to attain and thus saved it from the vulgar naturalism that threatened it.

We Russians cannot but take French Symbolism into account, if only because the new trend I spoke of above gives a decided preference to the Romance over the Germanic spirit. Just as the French sought a new, freer verse, the Acmeists strive to break the chains of meter by skipping syllables and by freer transposition of stress than ever before; and there are already poems written in a newly devised syllabic system of versification. The giddiness of Symbolist metaphors trained them in bold turns of thought; the instability of vocabulary, to which they became accustomed, prompted them to search in the living national speech for a new one with a more stable content; and a lucid irony, which has not undermined the roots of our faith—an irony which could not but appear if only from time to time in the Romance writers—has now replaced that hopeless German seriousness which our Symbolists so cherished. Finally, while we value the Symbolists highly for having pointed out to us the significance of the symbol in art, we cannot agree to sacrifice to it other methods of poetic influence and we seek the complete coordination of all of them. This is our answer to the question of the comparative "beautiful difficulty" of the two movements: it is harder to be an Acmeist than a Symbolist, just as it is harder to build a cathedral than a tower. And one of the principles of the new trend is always to take the line of greatest resistance.

German Symbolism, in the persons of its ancestors, Nietzsche and Ibsen, put forth the question of the role of man in the universe, the role of the invidivual in society, and settled it by finding some sort of objective goal or dogma which he was meant to serve. This showed that German Symbolism did not sense each phenomenon's intrinsic worth, which requires no justification from without. For us, the hierarchy of phenomena in the world is merely the specific weight of each of them, though the weight of the most insignificant is still immeasurably greater than the absence of weight, non-existence, and for that reason, in the face of non-existence, all phenomena are brothers.

We could not bring ourselves to force an atom to bow to God, if this were not in its nature. But feeling ourselves to be phenomena among phenomena, we become part of the world rhythm, accept all the forces acting upon us and ourselves become forces in our turn. Our duty, our feedom, our joy and our tragedy is to guess each hour what the next hour may be for us, for our cause, for the whole world, and to hurry its coming. And for our highest reward, never suspending attention for a moment, we dream of the image of the last hour, which will never arrive. But to rebel in the name of other conditions of existence, here, where there is death, is as strange as for a prisoner to break down a wall when in front of him there is an open door. Here, ethics becomes esthetics, expanding into the latter's sphere. Here, individualism in its highest effort creates community. Here, God becomes the Living God, because man felt himself worthy of such a God. Here, death is a curtain, separating us, the actors, from the audience, and in the inspiration of play we disdain the cowardly peeping of "What will happen next?" As Adamists, we are somewhat like forest animals and in any case will not surrender what is animal in us in exchange for neurasthenia. But now it is time for Russian Symbolism to speak.

Russian Symbolism directed its main energies into the realm of the unknown. By turns it fraternized with mysticism, then theosophy, then occultism. Some of its strivings in this direction nearly approached the creation of myth. And it has the right to ask the movement coming to take its place whether it can boast only of its animal virtues, and what attitude it takes toward the unknowable. The first thing that Acmeism can answer to such inquiry is to point out that the unknowable, by the very meaning of the word, cannot be known. The second, that all endeavors in that direction are unchaste. The whole beauty, the whole sacred meaning of the stars lies in the fact that they are infinitely far from earth and that no advance in aviation will bring them closer. He who conceives of the evolution of personality always within the conditions of time and space reveals a poverty of imagination. How can we remember our previous existences (if that is not a patently literary device), the time we were in the abyss, with myriads of other possibilities of being, of which we know nothing, except that they exist? For each of them is negated by our being and each in its turn negates it. The feeling of not knowing ourselves, childishly wise and sweet to the point of pain—that is what the unknown gives us. Francois Villon, asking where the most beautiful women of antiquity are now, himself answers with the mournful exclamation:

...Mais où sont les neiges d'antan!

And this allows us to feel the unearthly more strongly than whole tomes of discourse on which side of the moon houses the souls of the dead.... The principle of Acmeism is always to remember the unknowable, but not to insult one's idea of it with more or less likely conjectures. This does not mean that it denies itself the right

23

to portray the soul in those moments when it trembles, approaching another; but then it ought to shudder only. Of course, knowledge of God, the beautiful lady Theology, will remain on her throne, and the Acmeists wish neither to lower her to the level of literature, nor raise literature to her diamond coldness. As for angels, demons, elemental and other spirits, they are part of the artists's material and need not have a specific gravity greater than other images he chooses.

Any movement will experience a passionate love for certain writers and epochs. The loved ones' graves tie people together more closely than anything. In circles familiar to Acmeism, the names most frequently spoken are those of Shakespeare, Rabelais, Villon and Thèophile Gautier.[3] The choice of these names is not arbitrary. Each of them is a cornerstone of the edifice of Acmeism, a lofty exercise of one or another of its elements. Shakespeare showed us man's inner world; Rabelais—the body and its joys; Villon told us of a life which has not the slightest doubt in itself, although it knows everything—God, sin, death and immortality; Thèophile Gautier found in art worthy garments of irreproachable forms for this life. To unite in oneself these four moments—that is the dream which now unifies the people who so boldly call themselves Acmeists.

Apollo, No. 1, 1913, pp. 42-5.

THE READER

Poetry for man is one of the methods of expressing his personality and manifests itself by means of the word, the sole instrument that satisfies its requirements. Everything that is said about the poetic nature of some landscape or natural phenomenon merely indicates its suitability as poetic material, or hints at a very distant analogy in an animistic spirit between the poet and nature. The same applies to actions or feelings of man that are not embodied in the word. They may be beautiful, like impressions given by poetry, but they will not become it, because poetry scarcely includes everything beautiful that is accessible to man. No means of poetic phonetics will convey the true voice of a violin or flute, no stylistic devices will embody the brightness of the sun or the blowing of the wind.

Poetry and religion are two sides of the same coin. Both require spiritual labor from man. But not in the name of a practical goal, as ethics and esthetics do, rather in the name of a higher goal, unknown even to themselves. Ethics adapts man to life in society, esthetics strives to increase his aptitude for pleasure. Direction of man's rebirth as a higher type belongs to religion and poetry. Religion appeals to the collective. For its aims, whether the construction of a heavenly Jerusalem, universal praise of Allah, or the purification of matter in Nirvana, concerted efforts are essential, rather like the labor of polyps forming a coral reef. Poetry always appeals to the individual. Even where the poet speaks with the crowd, he speaks separately with each member of the crowd. Poetry requires of the individual the same thing religion does of the collective. First, recognition of its uniqueness and omnipotence, second, perfection of one's nature. The poet who has understood "the grasses' obscure scent," wants the reader to feel the same thing. He must act, so that "the astral book is clear" to everyone and "the sea wave speaks with him." For this reason, in moments of creation the poet should be master of some sensation unrealized before him, and valuable. This gives rise in him to a feeling of catastrophy, it seems to him that he speaks his last and the most important thing, without knowledge of which it would not even have been worth the world's coming into being. It is a most peculiar feeling, sometimes filling one with such trembling that it would hinder speaking, were there not the accompanying feeling of triumph, the sense that you are creating perfect combinations of words, like those that once raised the dead and demolished walls. These two feelings occur even in poor poets. Study of technique makes them appear more rarely, but produce greater results.

Poetry has always wished to dissociate itself from prose. By both typographic (earlier calligraphic) means, beginning each line with a capital letter, and acoustic means, the clearly-heard rhythm, rhyme, alliteration; stylistically, creating a special "poetic" language (the troubadours, Ronsard, Lomonosov), compositionally, attaining a special conciseness of thought, and eidolologically, in the choice of images. And everywhere prose has followed behind her, insisting that there is really no difference between them, like a poor man tormenting a rich relative with his friendship. Recently its strivings seems to have been crowned with success. On the one hand, it has, beneath the pen of Flaubert, Baudelaire, Rimbaud, gained the manners of fortune's favorite, on the other, poetry, remembering that the midwife is a necessary condition of its existence, tirelessly searches for newer and newer means of influence and has approached the forbidden sphere in Wordsworth's verse, Byron's composition, free verse, etc., and even in outline, since Paul Fort[1] prints his poems in lines like prose.

I think that it is impossible to find the exact boundary between prose and poetry, just as we will not find it between plants and minerals, animals and plants. However, the existence of hybrid individuals does not degrade the pure type. And in regard to poetry, its latest investigators have come to an agreement. In England, Coleridge's axiom still prevails defining poetry as "the best words in the best order." In France—the opinion of Théodore de Banville:[2] a poem is that which has been created and cannot be corrected. Mallarmé has sided with these two opinions, saying: "Poetry is everywhere there is the external intensification of style."

Expressing himself in the word, the poet always addresses someone, some listener. Often this listener is he himself, and here we have to deal with a natural split of personality. Sometimes it is a sort of mystical interlocutor, a friend or beloved not yet appeared, sometimes it is God, Nature, the People...

This is in the moment of creation. However, it is a secret to no one, much less the poet, that every poem finds itself a real, living reader among contemporaries, at times among descendants. This reader scarcely deserves the contempt poets have so often poured upon him. It is thanks to him that books are printed, reputations created, it was he gave us the opportunity to read Homer, Dante, and Shakespeare. Besides, no poet should forget that in regard to other poets, he is himself only a reader. However, we are all like the man who has learned a foreign language through textbooks. We can speak, but do not understand when people speak with us. There are innumerable manuals for poets, but manuals for readers do not exist. Poetry develops, movements are replaced by other movements while the reader remains always the same, and no one tries to illumine the corners of his dark reader's soul with the lamp of knowledge. This is what we shall be concerned with now.

First of all, every reader is deeply convinced that he is an authority; one because he has risen to the rank of colonel, another because he has written a book on mineralogy, a third because he knows that there is no real skill in it: "I like it—that means it is good, I don't like it—that means it is bad; for poetry is the language of the gods, ergo, I can judge it absolutely freely." That is the general rule, but in its more complex aspects, readers are divided into three basic types—naive, snobbish and ecstatic. The naive reader searches poetry for pleasant memories: if he loves nature, he censures poets who do not speak of it; if he is a socialist, a Don Juan or a mystic, he searches for poems in his specialty. He wants to find images familiar to him in verse, references to things he likes. He speaks little of his impressions and usually does not justify his opinions. In general he is rather goodnatured, though subject to fits of blind rage, like any herbivorous creature. He is common among critics of the old school.

The snob considers himself an enlightened reader: he loves to speak of the poet's art. Usually, he knows of the existence of some technical device and watches for it while reading a poem. It is from him that you will hear that X is a great poet because he introduces complex rhythms, Y, because he creates new words, Z, because he excites by means of repetitions. He expresses his opinions extensively and at times interestingly, but, considering only one, more rarely two or three devices, he inevitably errs in the most deplorable manner. He is found exclusively among critics of the new school.

The ecstatic loves poetry and detests poetics. In former times, he was found in other areas of the human spirit. He demanded the burning of the first doctors, anatomists, who dared to reveal the secret of God's creation. He was among the sailors who hissed the first steamship, because a seafarer must pray to the Virgin Mary to give a propitious wind and not burn some sort of firewood to make some wheels spin. Supplanted in every other place, he has remained only among readers of poetry. He speaks of the soul, the color and the taste of a poem, of its marvelous strength, or on the contrary, its sluggishness, of the poet's coldness or warmth. One rarely meets with him, for he has been supplanted increasingly by the first two types, even among the poets themselves.

A cheerless picture, is it not? And if poetic creation is the impregnation of one soul by another through the word, like natural impregnation, it recalls the love of angels for Cainites, or, what amounts to the same thing, mere bestiality. However, there can be another reader, a reader-friend. This reader thinks only of what the poet says to him, becomes as if he had written the given poem, remembers it through its intonations, its movements. He experiences the moment of creation in all its complexity and poignancy, he knows very well how all the poet's achievements are tied through technique and how its very perfections are a sign that the poet is marked by God's favor. For him the poem is precious in all its material charm, just as his beloved's spittle and a hairy chest is for the singer of psalms.[3] You won't deceive him with partial achievements or bribe him with an attractive image. A beautiful poem enters his consciousness as an immutable fact, changes him, determines his feelings and actions. Only on condition of his existence does poetry fulfill its conciliatory task of ennobling the human race. Such a reader exists, I at least have seen one. And I think that if it were not for man's stubbornness and negligence, many could become such.

If I were Bellamy,[4] I would write a novel on the life of the reader of the future. I would tell of readers' movements and their struggle, of enemy-readers denouncing poets' insufficient divinity, of readers like D'Annunzio's Gioconda,[5] of readers like Helen of Troy, to win whom one must supass Homer. Fortunately, I am not Bellamy, and there will be one less bad novel.

What the reader has a right to and, therefore, ought to demand of the poet will be the subject of this book.[6] But it will not teach poets to write verse, just as an astronomy textbook will not teach how to create heavenly bodies. However, for poets it may serve as a test of things already written, and in the moment preceding creation, provide the opportunity of weighing whether a feeling is sufficiently rich, an image ripened, or an emotion strong, or whether it would not be better to give oneself some liberty and save one's powers for a better moment. One ought to write, not when one can, when one must. The word "can"ought to be thrown out of all spheres of poetic investigation.

Delacroix said, "It is necessary to study tirelessly the technique of one's art, so as not to think of it in moments of creation." Indeed, it is necessary either to know absolutely nothing of technique, or to know it well. The sixteen-year-old Lermontov wrote "Angel" and only ten years later could he write a poem equal to it. But then "Angel" was unique, while all of Lermontov's verses from 1840 to 1841 are beautiful. A poem, like Pallas Athene, arisen from the mind of Zeus, sprung from the soul of the poet, becomes an individual organism. And, like every living organism, it has its anatomy and physiology. First of all we see the combination of words, the flesh of the poem. Their properties and qualities are the subject of stylistics. Then we see that these combinations of words, complementing one another, lead to a definite impression, and we notice the skeleton of the poem, its composition. Then we clarify for ouselves the entire nature of the image, that sensation which spurred the poet to creation, the nervous system of the poem, and thus master the eidolology. Finally (although all this is done simultaneously), our attention is attracted to the acoustical side of the verse (rhythm, rhyme, combination of vowels and consonants), which, like blood, flows in its veins, and we understand its phonetics. All these qualities are characteristic of every poem, the most brilliant and the most dilettantish, just as it is possible to dissect the living and the dead. But physiological processes in an organism occur only on condition of a certain perfection, and, having dissected the poem in detail, we can only say if everything is in it that should be, and in sufficient quantity for it to have lived.

The laws of its life, that is, the interaction of its parts, must be studied specially, and for this the way has yet hardly been prepared.

In *The Guild of Poets: Almanac* (II-III) (Berlin, 1923), pp. 98-107.

THE ANATOMY OF A POEM

Among the numerous formulas defining the essence of poetry, two stand out, proposed by poets themselves, poets who pondered the mysteries of their craft. Coleridge's formula: "Poetry is the best words in the best order." And Théodore de Banville's formula: "Poetry is that which has been created and, therefore, does not need alteration." Both these formulas are based on an especially clear sense of the laws by which words affect our consciousness. A poet is one who considers all the laws governing the complex of words he has chosen. One who considers only a part of these laws could be a prose artist, and one who considers nothing but the ideological content of words and their combinations would be a man of letters, a creator of business prose. The enumeration and classification of these laws is poetic theory. Poetic theory must be deductive, not based only on the study of works of poetry, just as a mechanic explains various constructions, and does not simply describe them. However, the theory of prose (if such a thing is possible) can be only inductive, describing the devices of one or another prose writer. Otherwise it would merge with poetic theory.

Besides, according to Potebnia's[1] definition, poetry is a linguistic phenomenon or a special form of speech. All speech is addressed to someone and signifies something that concerns both speaker and listener, and to the latter the speaker ascribes some characteristics found in himself. The human personality is capable of endless subdivisions. Our words are an expression of only a part of us, of one of our faces. We can tell of our love to the beloved woman, to a friend, in court, in a drunken company, to flowers, to God. Clearly, each time our tale will be different, since we change depending on the situation. Closely tied to this is the same sort of multiformity in the listener, since we also address only a certain part of him. Thus, addressing the sea, we can note its kinship with us or, on the contrary, its estrangement, ascribe to it concern for us, indifference or hostility. Description of the sea from the folkloristic, pictorial or geological point of view, often tied with address, is not relevant here, since, clearly, address in this case is merely a device, and the real interlocutor is someone else.

Since in every address there is some volitional starting point, the poet, in order that his words be effective, must clearly see the relation between speaker and listener and sense the conditions under which a connection between them is really possible. This is the subject of poetic psychology.

In every poem both parts of the general poetics supplement each other. Poetic theory may be compared to anatomy and poetic psychology to physiology. And the poem is a live organism, subject to examination—both anatomical and physiological.

Poetic theory may be divided into four parts: phonetics, stylistics, composition and eidolology. Phonetics investigates the acoustical side of verse, the rhythm, that is the alternations of raising and lowering the voice, the instrumentation, that is the quality of the connections between various sounds, the study of endings and the study of rhyme from its acoustical side.

Stylistics examines the impression produced by a word depending on origin, age, classification in one or another grammatical category, or place in the sentence, and also by a group of words, which form virtually a single whole, for example, a simile, a metaphor, etc.

Composition has to do with the ordered units of ideas, and studies the intensity and succession of the thoughts, feelings and images included in the poem. Here applies the study of stanzas, because one or another stanza is a great influence on the poet's train of thought.

Eidolology sums up the themes of poetry and the poet's possible relationships to those themes.

Each of these parts passes unnoticed into the next, and eidolology directly adjoins poetic psychology. One cannot draw sharp dividing lines, and one should not. In really great works of poetry, all four parts receive equal attention, they are mutually complementary. Such are Homer's epics, such is *The Divine Comedy*. Major poetic movements usually direct particular attention to some two of the parts, joining them together and leaving the other two in the background. Lesser ones single out only one part, sometimes even some one device included in its stock. I should point out, incidentally, that Acmeism, arisen in the last few years, presents as its basic requirement uniform attention to all four parts. The French poets who formed the now-disintegrated group, L'Abbaye,[2] adhere to the same requirement.

Let us try to conduct a test of this fourfold analysis on material taken from the sphere of that condensed poetry which serves as liturgy. Dionysius the Areopagite[3] recounts that angels, extolling God, exclaim: "alleluia, alleluia, alleluia." Basil the Great[4] explains that in human language this means: "Praise to Thee, O Lord!"[5] Our Old Believers sing: "alleluia, alleluia, praise to Thee, O Lord!" Among the Orthodox the word alleluia is repeated three times. Hence a great controversy.

In regard to phonetics we see in the singing of the Old Believers one line of trochaic heptameter with a caesura after the fourth foot, a line of integral meter and in it agitation fully corresponding to the purpose; the trochaic enneameter of the Orthodox inevitably breaks into two lines, hexametric and trimetric, owing to which the integrity of the appeal is lost. Moreover, since with any contiguity of long and short lines we always try to equalize our impression of them, singling out the short one and suppressing the long one, the angelic words gain the character of a sort of refrain, a supplement to the human ones, and are not equipollent to them.

In regard to stylistics, in the old wording we observe the correct replacement of a foreign word by a native one, as, for example, in the sentence, "*Avez-vous vu* Aunt Masha?" while in the new one, "Praise to Thee, O Lord!" is an absolutely unnecessary translation, like, "Drop by for our five o'clock at five o'clock."

In regard to composition, the old wording again has the advantage, owing to its trinomiality, much more akin to our consciousness than the tetranomiality of the new wording.

And in regard to eidolology, we feel in the old wording an appeal to all three persons of the Holy Trinity separately, while in the new, it is unknown to whom the fourth appeal applies.

We trust that the time will come when poets will weigh their every word with the same care as creators of religious canticles.

The Almanac *Draco* (Petersburg, 1921).

ON TRANSLATIONS OF POETRY

I

There are three methods for translating verse: by the first, the translator uses whatever meter and combination of rhymes happen to come into his head, his own vocabulary, often alien to the author, and at his personal discretion now lengthens, now shortens the original; clearly, such translation can only be called amateurish.

By the second method, the translator acts, for the most part, in the same way, but introduces a theoretical justification for his act; he assures us that if the poet being translated had written in Russian, he would have written in just that way. This method was very widespread in the eighteenth century. Pope in England, Kostrov[1] in our country translated Homer that way and enjoyed extraordinary success. The nineteenth century rejected this method, but traces of it remain in our own day. Even now some still think that it is possible to substitute one meter for another, for example, pentameter for hexameter, forego rhyme, introduce new images and so forth. The spirit preserved is supposed to justify everything. However, a poet worthy of the name uses precisely the form as the only means of expressing the spirit. I shall try to outline now how this is done.

II

The first thing that attracts the reader's attention and, in all probability, the most important, if often unconscious, basis for the creation of a poem is its idea or, more exactly, its image, since a poet thinks in images. The number of images is limited, evoked by life, and the poet is rarely their creator. Only in his relationship to them is his personality revealed. For example, the Persian poets thought of the rose as a living being, the medieval poets as a symbol of love and beauty; Pushkin's rose is a beautiful flower on its stem, Maikov's rose is always a decoration, an accessory; in Vyacheslav Ivanov the rose assumes mystical value, etc. Naturally, in all these cases both the choice of words and their combinations are essentially different. Within the bounds of the same relationship

34

there are thousands of nuances: thus, the comments of Byron's Corsair stand out against the background of the author's psychologically flowery description of him in their laconism and technical choice of expressions. In his gloss to "The Raven," Edgar Allan Poe speaks of an undercurrent theme, scarcely outlined, and for that very reason producing an especially powerful impression. If someone translating that same "Raven" were to transmit with greater care the external plot of the movements of the bird, and with less—the poet's longing for his dead beloved, he would have violated the author's conception and failed to complete the task he had taken upon himself.

III

Immediately after the choice of image, the poet is confronted with the question of its development and proportions. Both determine the choice of the number of lines and stanzas. In this the translator is obliged to blindly follow the author. It is impossible to shorten or lengthen a poem without at the same time changing its tone, even if the quantity of images is retained. Both laconism and amorphousness of image are determined by the conception, and each extra or missing line changes its degree of tension.

As for stanzas, each of them creates a particular train of thought, unlike the others. Thus, the sonnet, stating some proposition in the first quatrain, reveals its antithesis in the second, outlines their interaction in the first tercet and in the second tercet gives it an unexpected resolution, condensed in the last line, often even in the last word, for which reason it is called the key of the sonnet. The Shakespearian sonnet, with quatrains unconnected by rhyme, is supple, flexible, but devoid of sufficient strength; the Italian sonnet, with only feminine rhymes, is powerfully lyrical and stately, but of little use for narrative or description, for which the usual form is perfectly suited. In the ghazal, the same word, sometimes the same expression repeated at the end of every line (the Europeans incorrectly break it into two lines) creates an impression of gaudy ornament or incantation. The octave, extensive and spacious like no other form, is suitable for calm and unhurried narration. Even such simple stanzas as the quatrain and the couplet have their peculiarities which the poet takes into account, if only unconsciously. Moreover, for any sort of serious acquaintance with a poet it is essential to know what stanzas he preferred and how he used them. For that reason exact retention of the stanza is the duty of the translator.

IV

In the realm of style, the translator should really master the author's poetics in regard to this question. Each poet has his own vocabulary, often supported by theoretical considerations. Wordsworth, for example, insists upon using colloquial language. Hugo— upon employing words in their direct senses. Hérédia[2]—upon their precision. Verlaine, on the contrary, upon their simplicity and casualness, etc. One should also elucidate—and this is especially important—the character of the translated poet's similes. Thus, Byron compares a concrete image with an abstract one (a famous example is Lermontov—"The air as pure and fresh as a child's kiss"), Shakespeare—an abstract with a concrete image (an example in Pushkin—"A sharp-clawed beast, gnawing at the heart, is conscience"), Hérédia—a concrete with concrete ("Like a flock of falcons flown down from their native cliffs...the warriors and captains bid Palos farewell"); Coleridge draws the image of a simile from among the images of a given play ("and each soul sang, like that arrow of mine"); in Edgar Allan Poe the simile moves into development of image, etc. In poetry there are often parellelisms, complete, inverted, shortened repetitions, exact indications of time or place, quotations interspersed in the stanza, and other devices with special hypnotizing effects upon the reader. It is advisable to preserve them carefully, sacrificing less essential things. Besides, many poets have paid great attention to the semantic meaning of rhyme. Théodore de Banville even maintained that rhyme words, as the dominant ones, arise first in the consciousness of the poet and form the poem's skeleton: for this reason it is desirable that at least one of a pair of rhymed words correspond to the word at line-end in the original.

It is necessary to warn the majority of translators with regard to the use of such particles as "already," "only," "just," "you know," won't it?" etc. These all possess a powerful expressiveness and usually double the verb's effective power. One can avoid them, choosing among synonymous but non-homologous words, of which there are many in Russian, for example: "road—way," "Lord—God," "Love—passion," etc., or resorting to contractions, like "wind," "dreaming," "song," etc.

Slavonicisms or archaisms are permissible, but with great caution, only in the translation of old poets, who predate the Lake School and Romanticism, or of stylists like William Morris[3] in England or Jean Moréas in France.

V

Finally, there remains the acoustical side of verse: it is hardest of all for the translator to transmit. Russian syllabic verse is still too little developed to reconstruct French rhythms; English verse allows an arbitrary mixture of masculine and feminine rhyme, which is not characteristic of Russian. It is necessary to resort to relative transmission: to translate syllabic verse in iambs (sometimes trochees), to introduce regular alternation of rhymes into English verse, resorting here, where possible, to masculine rhymes only, as more characteristic of the language. Nevertheless, it is essential that this relative transmission be strictly adhered to, because it was not created by chance and, for the most part, really gives an adequate impression of the original.

Each meter has its own feeling, its own peculiarities and purposes: the iamb, as if going down stairs (the accented syllable being lower in pitch than the unaccented), is free, clear, firm and beautifully transmits human speech, the tension of the human will. The trochee, rising, winged, is always agitated and now anxious, now moved, now amused; its sphere is song. The dactyl, leaning on the first accented syllable and swinging the two unaccented ones as a palm tree does its top, is powerful, stately, speaks of the elements at rest, of the deeds of gods and heroes. The anapest, its opposite, is impetuous, fitful, it is the elements in action, the tension of inhuman passion. And the amphibrach, their synthesis, lulling and transparent, speaks of the peace of an existence divinely light and wise. Different measures in these meters also differ in their characteristics: thus, iambic tetrameter is most often used for lyric narration, pentameter—for epic or dramatic narration, hexameter—for discourse, etc. Poets often struggle with these characteristics of form, demand other possibilities of them and at times succeed in this. However, such a struggle always affects the image, and for that reason, it is essential to preserve its traces in the translation, strictly observing the meters and the measure of the original.

The question of rhyme has been of great interest to poets: Voltaire demanded acoustical rhyme, Théodore de Banville—visual; Byron readily rhymed proper names and used compound rhyme, the Parnassians—rich rhyme; Verlaine, on the contrary, used suppressed rhyme; the Symbolists often resort to assonance. The translator should determine the character of his author's rhyme and follow it.

Also extremely important is the question of the run-over of a sentence from one line to another, the so-called *enjambement*. Classical poets like Corneille and Racine did not permit this; the Romantics brought it into general use; the modernists have developed it to the extreme. In this too, the translator should consider the views of the author.

From all that has been said, clearly, the translator of a poet must be a poet himself and, besides that, a careful investigator and perceptive critic, who, selecting what is most characteristic for each author, allows himself to sacrifice the rest when necessary. And he must forget his own personality, thinking only of the personality of the author. Ideally, translations should not be signed.

One wishing to advance the technique of translation can go even farther: for example, maintain the rhymes of the original, render syllabic verse as such in Russian, find words for rendering characteristic modes of speech (British military language in Kipling, Laforgue's[4] Parisian jargon, Mallarmé's syntax, etc.).

Of course, for the ordinary translator this is by no means obligatory.

Let me repeat briefly what it is obligatory to observe: 1) the number of lines, 2) the meter and measure, 3) the alternation of rhyme, 4) the nature of the *enjambement* 5) the nature of the rhyme, 6) the nature of the vocabulary, 7) the type of similes, 8) special devices, 9) changes in tone.

These are the translator's nine commandments: since there is one less than those of Moses, I hope that they will be better observed.

in *Principles of Literary Translation* (Petersburg, 1919).

I

[**Valery Bryusov**. *Paths and Crossroads: Collected Poems.* Vol. 1. Moscow: Skorpion, 1908.]

Lately whole articles have been devoted to Bryusov, the best critics have been writing about him, and it would be strange in a short review to attempt to characterize his work, so complex and unified in its complexity. But then, another task presents itself to the critic: to note, if only in general outline, those peculiarities of form and thought which distinguish the second volume of *Paths and Crossroads* from the first. And most striking of all is the wholeness of the plan and the firm decision to follow the path of Symbolism, which in the first volume sometimes weakened with inclinations toward Decadence and Impressionism. Bryusov operates with only two quantities—"the self" and "the world" and in severe diagrams, devoid of anything fortuitous, gives the various possibilities of their interrelation. He reveals new horizons for elucidating the question of acceptance of the world, transferring events to a higher plane of thought, where the esthetic standard loses its validity and gives place to the ethical standard. At a wave of his hand, flowers again bloom in our world, which intoxicated the gaze of Assyrian kings, and passion becomes eternal, as in the times of the goddess Astarte.[1]

The world is again beautiful and more than redeems itself.

...And whether there is or not a road through the grave,
I was! I am! I do not need eternity!

The distinguishing feature of Bryusov's ballads is their nobility.

Even in the circles most hostile to him, Bryusov earned the reputation of a master of form. He shares the dreams of Mallarmé and René Ghil about the return of the word's metaphysical value, but resorts neither to neologisms nor intentional syntactic difficulties. Through severe selection of expressions, sharpened clarity of thought and brazen music of phrase he achieves results which were not always the lot of his French colleagues. The eternally unsubmissive word no longer fights with him; it has found its master.

Lately one often hears attacks on Bryusov from the most antithetical camps. They reproach him for pride, self-conceit, contempt for real life. There is nothing surprising in this. People are already long accustomed to consider poets officials of the literary department, and have long forgot that spiritually they descend from the line of Orpheus, Homer and Dante. Bryusov is blamed for having remembered that.

Speech (Rech'), May 29, 1908.

II

[Fedor Sologub. *Fiery Circle : Poems.* **Book VIII. Publication of the journal** *The Golden Fleece.*]

Sologub's poems have a strange property. You read them in magazines, newspapers, you are surprised at their refined form and you forget them in the day's commotion. But later, perhaps in a few months, when you are alone and sad, suddenly a certain strange and familiar melody sounds on the strings of your soul and you remember some poem by Sologub, read through once, but all whole. And none are completely forgotten. All of them have the ability of stars to appear at this or that hour of the nighttime silence.

I explain this by the fact that Sologub avoids the fortuitous, the pearls of his experiences are brought up from the depths, where all souls merge into one accord. In his work he follows the advice of Schopenhauer: to renounce the will for the sake of contemplation. But in his every phrase, in every image, one feels how difficult this victory was, and the sharp reader finds lightning bolts at every step, petrified, but still warm. Sologub's tranquillity wounds more painfully than the turbulence of others.

In *Homo Sapiens,* Przybyszewski[1] speaks in passing of a man who imagined he saw the broken wings of a big white bird. A few years ago that seemed the ideal of man's fate. A powerful flight upward, a relentless fall, and then the silence of despair.

But Sologub did not follow this path. In the valley of sorrow he discovered a tender, unbiting sun, and found sweetness in the

40

juice of bitter subterranean grasses. Here he invites men to admire his treasures: the blood-stained idol of Polynesian villages, the supple stalks of wormwood and the sinful crimson of the ruby. He is no longer lucid and powerful, striving toward God, he is a soothsaying wizard who has his paradise on the star Mair.[2] Having crossed the bounds of fire, where all living things perish, his work lives a differenct existence, it is like the leaden waters of a bewitched lake which reflects the whole world, but reflects it transfigured, and, looking into it, it seems that all else is shadow and raving madness.

Turning to the formal side of Sologub's work, first of all you note the complex mechanism of his devices. His themes are ever familiar and ever new: caressing death, love without desire, sorrow and an impulse toward revolt. But for each one there is a new image, words disturbing in their unexpectedness. Like all great artists, Sologub avoids calling things by their names; often he gives only one characteristic of some event, but one so powerful and apt that it replaces pages of description.

His verse, gentle and melodious, is devoid of both the brazen ringing of Bryusov's verse and the unexpected turns of Blok's. But then, he was less subject to the influence of the old masters; in him, together with the same fascination, one feels less literariness.

In the book *Fiery Circle* there are some old poems, and for this reason alone, less powerful ones. But they are successfully woven into the general structure of the book, and serve as ties, binding its separate elements.

The book is published as it should be published: beautifully and simply.

Speech September 18, 1908.

III

[Konstantin Balmont. *Only Love.* Second Edition (1908).]

So recently written, and already an historic book. Thus falls the lot of either very good or very bad books, and of course, *Only Love* belongs to the first category. In my opinion it most deeply reflects Balmont's talent, proud as the thought of a European, colorful as a southern tale, and pensive as the Slavic soul. In it he is that very Balmont-Arion[1] whom they rightly called by the ancient tender name of the mellifluous poet. And the readers of Balmont's latest works (are there many of them?) will read with sorrow this book, strangely beautiful, refined in thought and feeling, in which perhaps the germs of later decay already hide—the corruption of the virgin Russian word in the name of its wealth. There is something unmitigated in the melodiousness and imagery of these poems, but they are still timid, like a girl in the instant of her fall. Balmont said: "If I approach the abyss, lost in admiration of a star, / I will fall not regretting that I will land on stones." He has come immeasurably close to the star of pure poetry, and now the swiftness of his fall is merciless. *Only Love* concluded the brilliant morning of the renaissance of Russian poetry. At that time the formulas of a new life were only projected, of a literature united with philosophy and religion, of a poetry as guide of our actions. It was necessary to go over unexplored roads, to reveal hidden worlds in one's soul and to learn to look at things already known with a fresh and ehthusiastic gaze, like on the first day of creation. Balmont was one of the first and most insatiable discoverers, but his thoughts were not confined to the Promised Land, he delighted in the charm of the path. But then, no one's hands picked such dazzling flowers, in no one's curls rested such golden bees. It seemed that his muse was not subject to the laws of gravity. And justly, before all other "Decadents," he gained recognition and love.

But when the time came for creative work, and the swords were beaten into plows and hammers, Balmont turned out to be alien to everyone. Came the time of the great sunset.

And these confused wanderings-through the folklore of all lands and peoples which have occupied him recently, add nothing to his repute. There has been much talk about whether his talent would revive, his former love of the word and his intuitive understanding of its laws. An answer to this question we await from him alone.

Spring, No. 10, 1908.

IV

[Yury Verkhovsky. *Various Poems.* Moscow: Skorpion, 1908]

In this book there are "Melodies of Fet," "Variations on a theme of Pushkin," "Sonnets of Petrarch," and much else—only Yury Verkhovsky himself is missing. The poet was either unable or unwilling to express his soul. He is a student, not a creator, but perhaps precisely in this lies the peculiar charm of his book. Indeed, the last few years have brought poetry so many new words, images and devices that it is difficult for us to become absorbed in study of the old masters, to revive in our memory forgotten joys and sorrows. Verkhovsky helps us do this. He learned from Baratynsky, Yazykov, Delvig, Polonsky and Maikov[1] —and he was able to find features in their work not noticed before, familiar to us and enchanting. Less valuable are his imitations of contemporary poets: Vyacheslav Ivanov, Andrei Bely and others. Even if only because these poets are alive and speak for themselves, and their work is not in any need of reminder.

Verkhovsky loves and understands the Russian language. He avoids both French and Slavic turns of speech and uses Slavonicisms with great tact.

Unfortunately, one cannot say the same of the form. His poems, almost always complete in thought, often do not have a balance of images: they are sometimes too long, sometimes too short for their theme. In his verse one feels neither melodiousness nor animation and the prearrangement of effects is too evident. But then, there is in it that noble seriousness that comes only with disinterested and deep love for art.

Whether Verkhovsky ever reveals his true face or not—what difference does it make? He is alone in literature, his book will scarcely be successful in our time of ten thousand faiths, and this will serve as direct evidence of its value and necessity.

Speech, November 29, 1908

V

[Andrei Bely. *Urn: Poems.* Moscow: Grif, 1909.]

Of the whole older generation of Symbolists, Andrei Bely is the least cultured—not in the bookish culture of the academics, something of a Siamese order which is valued only because it is difficult to get, and few have it; in this culture he is strong, he writes both of "the philosopher of Marburg" and of "the golden triangle of Hiram,"[1] —but in the true culture of mankind, which teaches respect and self-criticism, grows into flesh and blood and puts its mark on every thought, every action of man. Somehow once cannot imagine that he was ever in the Louvre, that he read Homer... And I am judging now not by *Ashes* and not by *Cup of Blizzards*[2] God be their judge, but by the whole creative work of Andrei Bely, which I have been following for a long time and with interest. Why with interest will be apparent from what follows.

The poet Bely quickly assimilated all the subtleties of contemporary poetic technique. Thus the barbarian immediately accepts the fact that one should not eat fish with a knife, wear colored collars in the winter or write sonnets with nineteen lines (as one not unknown poet did recently). He uses free verse and alliteration and internal rhyme. But he cannot write a regular poem with clear and distinct images and without a bluster of unnecessary words. In this he is inferior even to the third-rate poets of the past, like Benediktov, Mei, or Karolina Pavlova.[3] And one can strongly argue against his understanding of iambic tetrameter, the meter in which almost all of *Urn* is written. Tracing the development of the iamb in Pushkin, we see that this great meter inclined more and more toward use of the fourth paeon,[4] the one which gives verse the greatest sonority. It is incomprehensible why Andrei Bely renounces such an important means of giving life to his often wooden verses.

But what is the charm of Andrei Bely, why does one even want to think and speak of him? Because there are themes in his work, and these themes are truly profound and unusual. He has enemies—time and space, and friends—eternity, the ultimate goal. He makes these abstract concepts concrete, contrasts them to his

44

personal "self"; they are for him real beings of his world. Combining the too airy colors of the old poets with the too heavy and harsh ones of contemporary poets, he achieves surprising effects, which prove that the world of his dreams really is magnificent: "Satin, scarlet roses, / Wistful, crystal fountain."

The reader will be dissatisfied with my review. He will certainly want to know if I am praising or reproving Andrei Bely. I will not answer this question. The time for conclusions has not yet come.

Speech, May 4, 1909.

VI

Vladimir Pyast. *Fence: Poems.* **M. O. Vol'f, 1909.**

In this book, one finds a few epigraphs from Edgar Allan Poe, and in literary circles they spoke of his influence on the young poet. But in my opinion, the latter is closer to the English pre-Raphaelites than to the great mathematician of the senses. The same pensiveness, the same absence of posing and natural nobility of line. But more softness perhaps, bordering sometimes on diffusiveness, the obscurity of unreasoned mysticism. This is generally the distinctive characteristic of the book in question—the weariness of an experienced, inspired soul, with which thought does not keep pace.

Thought, as a literary device, is kept especially in the background in Pyast. He even seems to flaunt his attitude towards it, creating poems where there is nothing but image, an impassioned transport. His experiences amount to only seconds, but how lucid those seconds are. And his poems, often devoid of structure, live like a loosed arrow, in the piercing thrill of flight. Sometimes the feeling reaches such intensity that it creates an almost visible copy of the instant. Such is the poem beginning: "We froze in a solemn vow, / We understood that we are children of the Lord."

As a technician Pyast lacks much: his favorite hyperdactyllic rhymes irritate the ear, the verse is not flexible, is occasionally flaccid, and the poverty of the language is especially painful. But on the other hand other riches lead you to imagine yourself in a curiosity shop among all those poisoned arrows, sea-urchins, candlesticks and broken Greek vases.

And I am happy for Pyast that his book has the shortcomings which exclude it from newsstands in railroad stations.

Speech, July 6, 1909.

VII

Valerian Borodaevsky. *Poems.* **SPb. : Ory, 1909.**

If I am not mistaken, Borodaevsky[1] appears in print for the first time, but even so one cannot consider his book premature.

One senses that behind his poems stand years of thought, years of persistent creative work. He has something to say, and he wants to say it as well as possible. Thus the refinement of his forms, a series of new meters and new stanzas.

Almost every one of his poems is written on a truly artistic theme, and reveals to us the obsessions of a strange, mocking and frightened soul. One would like to adopt the following lines from the book itself as its epigraph: "And why so cold? And why so soon? / And why are the roads covered with snow?"

As a mystic, Borodaevsky does not know the benevolent Christ of the sunny fields of Judea; a Russian Christ is dear to him, "oppressed by the burden of the cross," with lips too parched to give blessing. This Christ sees the most agonizing doubts, the blackest sins, and he forgives, not because he loves, but because he understands. The Magi did not bear him gifts of gold, and he does not have a paradise of white lillies.

In conformity with this, Borodaevsky's poems are dull in tone and unwholesomely refined in their intermittent rhythms. He feels neither lines nor colors. As for syntax, his breath, short and quick like that of a man dead tired, does not permit him to create the long, majestic periods, the refined expressions, toward which the Russian language is so disposed. And the absence of literariness in his verse, the failure to treat thought as the basis for a poem is terribly annoying. His seriousness sometimes even provokes a smile, for example in the poem "In the Museum."

There is an introduction by Vyacheslav Ivanov, magnificent in style and image, an example of what criticism should do according to Oscar Wilde: extend the subject in question and give it a fascination which it perhaps does not possess.

Speech, September 21, 1909.

VIII

Sergei Gorodetsky. *Russia: Song and Ballads.* Moscow: Sytina, 1909.
Valerian Borodaevsky. *Poems.* Spb.: Ory, 1909.
Boris Sadovskoy. *Late Morning. : Poems.* Moscow, 1909.
Ivan Rukavishnikov. *Poems, Book Six.* Spb.

On a cool spring morning, it is good to walk alone along a path, not expecting any meetings. The sun on the grass, on your clothes, the slightly damp earth sinking softly underfoot—and then you involuntarily start to sing, dancing and clicking your heels, swinging your shoulders and waving your cane. To sing, of course, without words—you don't remember words on such a marvellous morning. This is not the stately hymn of maturing ideas for a creative work, like those Schiller had, it is the spontaneous rapture of being—the neighing of horses swimming, the head-long flight of the skylark, the frantic leaps of a playing dog. You are carried away with a song like that, and you don't need to get anything else from it. But Sergei Gorodetsky conceived the strange idea of putting words to it, made a book of the resulting verses and called it *Russia,* the fifth book of his poems. I read it with a feeling of sweet melancholy and even greater embarrassment, for the author, rushing to put words to a melody that was still growing, didn't have time to evaluate them, or even to pick suitable ones. It is absolutely out of the question to speak of style, interesting structure or technical precision here. Gorodetsky forgot everything he ever knew, or should have known as a poet. The book is called *Russia*, but there is no Russia here—there are only light feet, cocked army caps and smiling red lips. Whether this has anything to do with literature I don't know, but with poetry, I think it does.

Valerian Borodaevsky's book of poems is in a completely different vein. You feel in it a knowledge of many metrical secrets, alliteration, assonance; the rhymes in it are first tender and limpid like a distant echo, then clear and confident like clashing silver shields. But a deep dissatisfaction with the world and a burning thirst for something different do not allow the poet to concentrate on his images, they are often not well thought out and have an annoyingly accidental quality. And therefore in the highest and most beautiful notes of his song, you hear the tremor of approaching hysteria.

True, he does not sing much, he prefers to speak of his

visions with a simple and frightening voice. First he sees God, lighting his cigarette by a shack and staring out into the barren steppe, then as in the mines, "the grayish necks and hanging lips of the prison horses tremble." Sometimes he is solemn, and then words escape his lips which are convincing in their unexpectedness.

> Seal of the Antichrist! Judas! Day of Judgement!
> You are always the same, —icon of Byzantium.
> But your fire is brighter! —They are forging and
> burning hearts...
> O, sages... Deaf-mute slaves!

Vyacheslav Ivanov has reason to call him "a Byzantine at heart" in his preface; for Borodaevsky, Christianity is the right to suppress and damn, for him Passion Week has not yet ended with the Resurrection.

His most typical colors are black and red, as if for someone who looks through tightly closed eyelids.

But perhaps it is exactly this repressed cruelty which makes his work deeply individual, despite the noticeable influences of Tyutchev, Fet and Vyacheslav Ivanov.

Boris Sadovskoy[1] is chiefly a prose writer. In his book *Late Morning* he has collected poems from the last five years, but you feel no difference in them, neither improvement nor development.

He adopted a particular manner of writing immediately, completely grammatical and unpretentious, and it seems he does not plan to deviate from it one iota.

Let Bryusov, like a hunter, lie in wait for secrets in the night-time labyrinths of passion and thought, let Ivanov raise the shining banner of Christ-Dionysus, and Blok now madly grieve for the Beautiful Lady, then madly laugh at her—Sadovskoy looks at them suspiciously. "In the foggy haze of the frost the creak of runners, the barking of dogs, the groaning of the water-carrier"— these themes will never change, one can go through one's whole life with them.

I do not think that anyone could bring himself to reproach a poet for such modesty. If he can do only a little, at least he is quite aware of his powers. A few stanzas inspired by Bryusov and Bely only support my idea, they sound so hesitant, so artlessly imitative of the peculiarities of both models.

Of course, Boris Sadovskoy will not do for the roles of conquistador, champion, bearer of gold bullion and diamond diadems to fill the treasure-house of poetry, but he has made a pretty good colonist for the regions already tamed and cleared.

If Gorodetsky sings, Borodaevsky speaks and Sadovskoy writes, then Ivan Rukavishnikov is daring. Undoubtedly talented, hard-working, thoughtful, he is absolutely devoid of the poet's sense—taste. Sometimes this even helps hims: he wanders along a narrow ledge like a lunatic and really does find sweet smelling lawns, silver fields, and bewitched lands. But more often—oh, how often this happens! —he falls painfully, and not into the abyss, but only into the mud; and his poems are spotted with blots of hideous prosaisms.

In his book there are poems in the shape of a chalice, a sword, a cross and a triangle, an imitation of the Alexandrian poets. There are many new metres and new stanzas in it. Characteristic of Rukavishnikov is the frequent repetition of some word or expression, giving his images a persistent character.

And in his works you often encounter themes of the occult, treated not deeply, but originally.

His book is material for poets, and rich material—but it would be awful to call its author a poet.

Apollo, No. 1, 1909.

IX

The Almanac *Death*. **SPb., 1909.**
Pavel Sukhotin. *Asters.* **Moscow, 1909.**
Vladimir Pyast. *Fence: Book of Poems.* **SPb., 1909.**
Sergei Krechetov. *The Flying Dutchman: Poems.* **Moscow, 1910.**

Recently the question of the revival of the epic has occupied many Russian poets. Did a few decades' experience with Symbolism turn out to be enough for a detailed development of eternal images, for great and confident strides in poetic thought, or did our organism not take the saving venom of Decadence and did we return from whence we came—how are we to know? It is painful to speak of the second possibility. But in the first case, contemporary poets accept the challenge of the old, compete with them on their own ground and with their own weapons.

After "City of Women" and "The Last Day," which are epics in the French sense of the word (i.e., simply big poems), Valery Bryusov printed the romantic epic "The Fulfilled Promise" and dedicated it to the memory of Zhukovsky.[1] Sergei Solovvev wrote an epic in hexameters, Kuzmin—the lyric epic "The New Rolla"[2] about life in the thirties of the last century (only excerpts of it have appeared in print). And so it is even more interesting to note Petr Potemkin's[3] attempt to write an epic of contemporary life in iambic tetrameter without stanzas, as Pushkin wrote them (the Almanac *Death*, "Eve," and epic by Petr Potemkin).

But alas, this attempt remains merely an attempt. In Potemkin's epic there are some truly profound allusions, some truly picturesque descriptions, but it lacks the most important thing—a successful idea and a well-conceived plan.

The story if about Boris, a young man whose soul is exhausted by constant fear of death. The author attributes this to an "absurd childhood"—a boring description vaguely reminiscent of Oblomov's youth[4] —and apparently does not even suspect that fear as well as love is a primordial characteristic of man's soul. Boris tries to escape from it into a world of dreamy visions and develops his ability to control his dreams at will. But when the image of a woman appears in them—first of a prostitute with coal-black brows, then the Princess Tamara, then Cleopatra (both the latter from Lermontov and Pushkin, according to the author)[5] — there is a crisis in Boris' life. Eternal Eve entices him with unheard of happiness, but demands an unheard of payment as well—voluntary death. Boris forgot the sweet and dreadful Ancient Name, and when he remembered it, there was only one thing left for him—flight from a sixth-story window.

First of all, Petr Potemkin's hero is unsuitable for an epic. He is not typical of our times (let us at least remember the recent revolution), and he has neither the internal strength, nor that complexity of emotional experience which gives value to the "solitary" type of Huysmans' novel, des Esseintes.[6] He is simply lethargic, and since he is essentially the only character in the epic, he communicates to it the same quality of lethargy.

The verse of the epic is distinguished by its clarity and comparative terseness, but it lacks sonority. Logical caesurae, not always internally justifiable, hamper its flow; the overabundance of the fourth paeon weakens it. There are almost no examples of the second paeon, the greatest of the variants of the iamb.[7]

"Eve" is Potemkin's second epic, and in comparison with the first, it is undoubtedly a step forward. But it still seems that this typical lyric poet has but few of the qualities essential for writing big things.

When you open the first book of poetry by an unknown poet—and Pavel Sukhotin[8] is really little-known—you involuntarily ask yourself: what new problems will he try to touch upon, what images govern his soul, what sort of attitude does he have toward the world, toward himself, what sort of pose does he adopt. You do not expect any sort of fulfillment—but promise, hints at promise even, and you forgive in advance everything but insipidity. And it is often sad, as in this case, when you get no answer to your questions.

Not one poem in Pavel Sukhotin's book sticks in your memory, not one stands out among the rest. In almost every one there are slips, there are apt expressions as well, but one wants to attribute both to the general endowments of the author, rather than to specifically poetic gifts. He is undoutedly "literary" and has taste. The crimson sunsets of the mysterious suns in the poems of Andrei Bely, whom he imitates somewhat, have become flatter and simpler in his verse. Now it is no longer necessary to climb to the snowy heights for them, they can be seen from any balcony. The sharp lines of the landscapes of Bunin and Pavel Sukhotin have become carefully retouched photographs. From the rhythmic standpoint his verses are uninteresting and often unsuccessful.

Perhaps Pavel Sukhotin is very young, perhaps he has not found himself yet? We shall hope so, despite the fact that boldness of approach is characteristic of talented youth and in *Asters* there is none.

In *Fence*, Vladimir Pyast's book of poems, there is both the daring of youth and the wise caution of a real worker. He loves hyperdactylic rhymes, changes the usual rhyme alternations of the sonnet, creates new stanzas. From the dates of his poems you can see that he does not write often, but waits for his moods to crystallize, clothed in the single, inevitable images and rhythms.

51

He is a lyric poet and the situations of his poems are uncomplicated, the figures and landscapes cloaked in the light smoke of reverie. There is a God, but He is only the state of a higher, blessed enlightenment. He is "the whole, personal, thrice-single 'self'." There are angels as well, but they too are only a state of the human soul on the road to perfection, states possible even in our world. In moments of despair the poet remembers them with a sort of deeply intimate sadness, like something lost not too long ago. The path to perfection is love and of course, love of woman. For this, Vladimir Pyast has word-hymns, word-flowers.

> Shy, tender, luminous, it looks with open eyes,
> Born of virgin soil, burned with a secret, womanly.
> In it is reflected, in it is born, with songs and caresses,
> Everything extraordinary, everything harmonic,
> everything infinitely universal.

The themes of Vladimir Pyast are the rosy reflections of Coming Dawns, and his damning arrogant poems from the section "To Ananka"—nor more than a pose—are successful, if you please, objectively, but are not at all characteristic of him. Not in vain is one of them called "Diaboli Manuscriptum." And what's a devil to Pyast!

In the first centuries of Christianity, when ecstasy was just as usual as scepticism is now, there were almost no general prayers, excluding the ones in the Old Testament, and every member of society would instinctively create his own address to God, sometimes of one sentence, or of two or three words. But then the words were joined together like the atoms of a diamond; it was said of them that earth and sky would pass before one word of the Scriptures would change. And the latest creators of prayers gathered them in garlands, already given value by the centuries.

In Vladimir Pyast there are such words, come as if from without: "We sank in a solemn embrace, / We understood that we are the children of God." Or: "...But why now do I kiss the dust of the mountain, / Where Thy voice did ring, thrown back by a loud echo?" Or: "...and I shall be, like a park, all filled with Thee..."

But Vladimir Pyast lives in our time, he cannot pray, he has to write poetry. And so, in order for poetry to come out, he makes up artificial lines to stick in between the inspired ones, he mixes poetry with literature. What results is a showcase of Tait diamonds,[9] where among masses of artificial stones, they assure us there are real ones as well. Literature is law-bound and wonderful, like a constitutional government, but inspiration is an autocrat, fascinating in that is living soul is above iron laws. I reproach the muse of Vladimir Pyast for fearing to be autocratic, although she has a right to be.

Of course, what I have just said should not influence a favorable appraisal of Vladimir Pyast's book. Though among the young swans of Russian Symbolism he is not the strongest, or the proudest and most handsome—he is the most mellifluous.

In Sergei Krechetov's book,[10] there is a poem "The Youngest Judges." In it he reports that they pronounced their inimical judgement upon him; that his chisel chases cold stanzas and makes their steel into icy armor; that he dreams of the sacred towers of Medina, and so many other interesting and awful things. And at the end he says:

> So! I am not a poet! But my crimson robes,
> I'll not take off to the market, joking and laughing,
> I'll lay at the feet of the queen invisible to you
>> Both pain and rapture.

And so, the whole thing is in the queen. Perhaps he is an occultist and secured the love of the queen Cleopatra—but why does he write poems then, and not quietly occupy himself with some sort of involutions? Perhaps he is a mystic and dreams of the Eternal Feminine, but once again—why does he write poems then, and not read papers at the Religio-Philosophical Congress? Obviously his queen is his artistic ideal. In that case Sergei Krechetov is sadly mistaken in thinking that she is invisible—she is well known to every high school student. Bryusov embraced her, and Aleksei Tolstoy, and Maeterlinck[11] and even (oh, horror!) Lensky[12] and Roslavlev.[13] It is a story right out of the *Decameron*.

Actually, the images of every poem by Krechetov are borrowed from some other poet.

The borrowing of whole lines are not uncommon, and not chance lines, but those which define the mood; so, in a famous poem by Aleksei Tolstoy, the line "And all this happened once before," in Krechetov reads "All this happened once before." You cannot defend yourself against chance, but in these two poems the images are similar as well.

Besides that, Krechetov is not familiar with the most elementary rules of stylistics. For example, here is an excerpt from the poem "The Accursed Tower":

No one knows if long
The gray-haired king lived in that tower.

Like a May day, fresh and sweet,
His young daughter bloomed.

Once, possessed by a demon,
He became drunk wthi sinful ardor.

Hiding in the gloom, like a thief in the night,
He stole past into her chamber.

The king destroyed his dear daughter,
He loved her but one night... etc.

The brevity of *Diary of Events*[13] and philosophizing to boot. And the author thinks he can make a thing like that pass for an aromatic legend of the Middle Ages!

However many shortcomings there are in Sergei Krechetov's book, justice demands we note the merits as well. First of all, the easy and confident verse, especially in anapestic meters. Then, ringing, unexpectedly pleasing rhymes.

Here is a stanza from the poem "The Flying Dutchman," as a little example of the positive side of Sergei Krechetov's verse.

Born to the sea, a favorite of Fortune,—
If, on the heights of the darkening masts
Above me, blue lights flare.

Apolloe, No. 2, 1909.

X

The Journal *Scales*, No. 9, 1909. Moscow.
The Journal *Island,* No. 2, 1909. SPb.

In No. 9 of *Scales*[1] a series of poems by Mr. Ellis,[2] the well-known translator and critic, is printed. It is odd to see that the man who appropriated the brazen language of Dante and the snake-like grace of Baudelaire, who boldly defended the canons of Symbolism from its enemies and at times even from its friends, turned out to be pale, artificial and quite frankly dull in his own poems. He does not think in words and images as poets do, he muses like a theoretician, and his musings are directed towards the field of mystical and occult philosophy, a waterless waste where flowering oases are so rare. But unaware of this, with the naivete of a hyperborean Symbolist, he writes of stigmata, thorns, and burning wounds. Words aromatic in reference to SS. Sebastian, Francis of Assisi, Benedict, but in reference to Mr. Ellis, they are a bit strange. Both stigmata and thorns here are abstract, and symbolism turns to allegory, because it goes not from the real to the other-worldly, but the other way around. Bryusov is the one who, when he wants to dress in armor, puts on the mask of a knight as well. Mr. Ellis' verse is flaccid and boneless; one simply should not start an anapest with the words *no lish'* [but only] . . . , but he writes: *No lish' k zemle, iznemogshi, sklonilas'...*

The themes of his verse are interesting, the emotional experiences are deep, but in order to handle them, you need a great talent, and Mr. Ellis does not have it.

The second number of *Island*[3] contains Annensky's poems "It happened at Wallen-Kosk" and "Balloons." What actually happened at Wallen-Kosk, what attracted the attention of the poet?

Why nothing. "A light rain fell from the damp clouds," after a sleepless night they yawned until they cried, and a Finn threw a wooden doll down the waterfall for half a ruble. But... "there is such a sky, such a play of sunbeams that the heart pities the doll's suffering more than its own." He found the word. There is suffering, one's own, and other people's, and that of others is more dreadful, more pitiable. For Annensky, to create is to go out to the sufferings of others, to cry with other people's tears, shout with other people's mouths, to teach his own mouth silence and his soul nobility. But he is greedy and cunning, he has the moon's drunken eyes, to use Nietzsche's expression, and he always returns to his own wound and reopens it, because it is only thanks to it that he is able to create. Thus, every pilgrim must have his hut with half-obliterated spots of someone's blood in the corner, where he can come to learn horror and anguish.

"Children's balloons, fathers' money, buy balloons,gentle-men!"—let the cry ring louder than all these Yaroslavtsy, these Petersburg bourgeois... or these Parisian *camelots*[4] on the wet pavement, under the smoky sky, and of course, not on the festival of the vernal Dionysia... So much more painful, so much more astonished will be the glance of a person left alone for a moment.

Annensky's verse is supple, everything in it has the intonation of ordinary speech, but there is no singing. His syntax is just as nervous and rich as his soul.

Apollo, No. 3, 1909.

XI

Konstantin Mikhailovich Fofanov. *After Golgotha.* **SPb., 1910.**
Vasily Cholba. *In My Dreams... Near Life: Poems, Aphorisms.*
SPb., 1910.
Evgeny Yantarev. *Poems.* **Moscow, 1910.**
Iosif Simanovsky. *New World: Poems.* **Bobruisk, 1910.**
Dmitry Rem, Aleksei Sidorov. *Poems.* **Moscow, 1910.**

Long, long ago, people liked to call Konstantin Fofanov the first Russian Decadent. They even published him in *Northern Flowers*.[1] But obviously this happened by some tactical scheme of the early leaders of Modernism, for there is absolutely no reason to suppose that Fofanov had an inkling of the great revolution in Russian art that took place in the Nineties. He is the typical imitator of the "school" of Apukhtin, Nadson and Frug.[2]

The same, perhaps the only, failure to understand the rules of rhythm and style in the annals of poetry, the same wordy cliches, worn to despair, the same circle of ideas, near and dear to the ordinary man in the street of the Eighties. *After Golgotha* is a mystery-epic. In flaccid and clumsy verse, it relates several well-known legends of Christ and the Virgin Mary's descent into Hell, passages from the Apocalypse. Perhaps Fofanov heard of those who once formed a society of religious research and wanted to join them. How does he do it? Well, here:

The earth is insignificant, the earth is transient;

56

And the cross of Golgotha is its lighthouse...
But the heart loves and believes dimly,–
That life–immortality and death–is not gloom.

What can one add to this? Really only that "The Volga falls into the Caspian Sea."

Vasily Cholba reminds one of K. Fofanov in many respects, but he is much more talented and cultured. It is obvious from his poetry that he knows both Yazykov and Alexei Tolstoy, probably, and even Heine. His old cliches don't worry one, they are almost always appropriate and lend his muse a quality of languor, which is a little tedious, but nevertheless suits his muse. His images can be daring without being garish. For example, in the poem "I sailed across the sea," he adds an interesting new touch to the theme of travel:

And I understood then, that a single
Distant dream enchants us, that it warmed my soul,
That my poor antipode, like me, yearns
For a land–my native soil–to him unknown.

His rhythms are not banal; the sonnets are constructed properly. He can write blank verse, a great rarity in our day; he knows secrets which allow him to unexpectedly replace rhymes with assonance in the middle of a poem. It is too bad really, that the accent in his poems often does not fall on the words it should according to the sense.

To the reader for whom expressions like "trembling bliss, the silvery moon, the sweet cup of love," and so forth still mean something, the poems of Vasily Cholba may give real pleasure. But if the reader is not a complete cretin, he must indignantly turn away from the aphorisms, ungrammatical, pretentious, and shallow, which have been appended to the book.

In the even flow of quotidian thoughts,
In the dead calm of lonely nights,
Somewhere in the lost, far, far days,
In days forever stilled, wrathless,
There was always something anxiously recalled...

This is the first poem that turned up in Evgeny Yantarev's

book. It is impossible to read it or discuss it.

Just try to literally think of nothing, to look and not see what is around you. In ninety-nine out of a hundred cases, it will not work. But Yantarev's poems bring you close to that repellent Nirvana of cheap furnished rooms. If the poems of Zinaida Gippius, also often written without colors, images, or mobile rhythm, resemble a sick pearl, then Yantarev's poems resemble soggy twilight seen through an uncleaned window, or a sticky whitish spider web on torn wall paper, in a corner with cockroaches.

It is awkward for me to discuss Iosif Simanovsky's book in an article entitled "Letters on Russian Poetry."[4] For it was not so long ago that Lev Tolstoy, reading in a pamphlet by Igor Severyanin the lines "Stick the corkscrew into the springy cork, and women's looks won't be so timid," was sadly surprised at the state to which Russian poetry had come, as if poetry were somehow responsible for the impossible freaks of literary imposters.

Iosif Simanovsky has supplied his book with a preface. In it, after a completely incoherent account of the "ideas" of his book, after cries that "the instant," taken in itself is "endless, eternal," that "the evening turns into a symbol of the world," and other Symbolist toys from the nursery, he quite rightly says that "not technique, but the originality of the undertaking and the images created can be a guarantee of talent in a young poet."

But alas, there are no images at all in *New World;* it is impossible to create them by such primitive methods as beginning nouns with capital letters; and originality in this book, if we are to ignore some badly understood Andrei Bely, lies only in a certain type of peculiar, wild absurdity.

After all, if a young poet runs a ring through his nose or walks backwards, it is still impossible to call this originality, promising for Russian literature. Worst of all, Iosif Simanovsky does not know Russian literature at all. Instead of *"bilsia,"* he writes *"biyalsia,"* instead of *"korchakh"—"korchak," "izgas,"* instead of *"pogas;"* in his works, one sees expressions like "pulse beats," "freezing in a writhing coil," "thirsty cry."

His only excuse is that the book was published in Bobruisk.[5]

Under the title *Toga Praetexta*,[6] Dmitri Rem and Aleksei Sidorov published their poems together in one book. One can explain such a combination by the fact that both of them have too few poems. So, the first has 27 pieces, the second, only 21. But one ought to discuss them separately.

Dmitri Rem... But here I want to make a digression. It is so dull to write reviews, both laudatory and querulous, with technical expressions and without.

It would be possible to write analyses, but who are you trying to write them about now? About three or four authors, not more. You would like to answer the poets who send their poems for comment with something of your own, dear and well-worn, to respond like an echo to the call of their dreams and not be, in the end, like Belinsky next to Pushkin, Sancho Panza next to Don Quixote...

Dmitri Rem I shall discuss on his merits. He is above all delicate, and deep and refined in his delicacy. He can say:

> Each day sharp autumn sorrows
> Pierced my heart.
> Each day my lips whispered:
> Thy kingdom come!

This delicacy leads him to a knowledge of the secret and joyous meaning of earthly expanses. "It is so good... Such a sleep they sleep / Come from the east to the sunset, / Tired, silent wanderers."

And it forces him to deny or detest the immortality of the soul:

> I am alone in the silence of the hall,
> And she will not be with me...
> Don't be sad, she is tired,
> And the tired need peace...
>
> But why is the final delirium
> Clouded with persistent fear?
> You forgot the priest in black?
> He told her that there is no death.

But this very delicacy subordinates him to other, more fully developed poets of delicacy.

Here is a line inspired by Blok: "With radiant heart I welcome Thy coming."

And here, from Kuzmin: "We drank tea from pale blue glasses..."

Aleksei Sidorov has entitled his section "First Poems." If these really are his first attempts, one can place some hopes in him. He imitates Valery Bryusov not at all badly and Andrei Bely even more successfully. However, for an imitation of the first he has neither the technique, the temperament, nor the taste (where Bryusov has a David, he has a Semiradsky),[7] and for an imitation of the second, the daring and freshness of invention by which the poetry of Bely is mainly held together.

In his book there are childish lines, trick lines, but he generally feels rhythm, loves rhyme and writes poems not because he wants to, but because he must.

Apollo, No. 6, 1910.

XII

Teffi. *Seven Fires: Poems.* **Spb.: Shipovnik, 1910.**
Daniil Ratgauz. *Ennui of Being: Poems.* **SPb.: Volf.**
Konstantin Podovodsky. *Summit Lights: Poems.* **Moscow, 1910.**

In Teffi's poems one enjoys most of all their literary quality, in the best sense of the word. A book like this could have appeared in French, and then some of the poems from it would have probably, and quite rightly, ended up in the Walch *Anthology.*[1] The poetess speaks not of herself, nor of what she loves, but of whom she might have been and of what she might have loved. Hence the mask, which she wears with solemn grace and, it seems, a just perceptible smile. This greatly reassures the reader, and he is not afraid to be taken in with the author.

Teffi loves the Middle Ages, and knows it for what Verlaine knew it to be—vast and delicate. Besides, she knows the tales of the Middle Ages, but not the sugary didactic ones, or the tastelessly ornamental ones you find in Tennyson, but the authentic, elegantly simple ones like those in Perrault, Mme. d'Aulnoy,[2] and other storytellers of the seventeenth century.

> Starving children on twisted legs,

A limp dandelion by a dusty stump!
And an old bird, gone blind in the cage!
I'll tell! I know! Listen to me!

In the sapphire tower of a golden palace
Queen Gulda with downcast eyes,
For the carpet of the throne of Lord God
Embroiders the ruby pattern of happiness.

Seven mountain deer humbly serve her,
They blink their emerald eyes, snort,
Paw the ground and wait for orders.
Wait to go where the downcast eyes direct...etc.

Teffi deals less successfully with the themes of Assyria and Babylon. The desire to find in them a beauty other than the beauty of ornamentation and to link it to our own experiences seems to be too exotic. You somehow don't believe in Queen Shammuramat, and the slave Atoraga, and the Mountains of Sindzhar, perhaps only because these names sound so unusually and unpleasantly harsh in Russian. Anna Comnena, after writing the biography of her father, Emperor Alexius, apologized to her readers for having had to destroy the noble rhythm of the Greek language with references to the coarse and dissonant names of the crusaders.[3] Our poetess, apparently, is less sensitive to the rhythm of the Russian language.

In the country there are shopkeepers who only know how to read and cannot write. I believe Ratgauz[4] is one of them. Otherwise he would not have had the nerve to give us the thoughts and feelings of backward youths of sixteen in tediously ungrammatical poems:

There is no joy in earthly love,
No bliss in earthly strivings,
And dimmer grows the light of happiness,
Paler the spectre of perfection.

How wretched are all our dreams,
How futile all our hopes,
As in the whirlwind of eternal vanity
We, like specks of dust, are imperceptible!

61

In this excerpt is the whole of Ratgauz. Already the unpleasantly polished verse shows that he is completely indifferent to the theme he has touched on; the uninteresting, overworked idea reveals the clumsiness of the author in his choice of other people's feelings, and the drab words—a complete lack of poetic originality; and when we learn from other poems that he considers himself a poet and believes that although generations may be long forgotten the songs are not, you feel like saying of him, in the words from his own piece "The Dreamer," which is appended to the end of the volume, that "...these men, callous by nature, stuffing their littlebrains with other people's wit, speaking other's words... these none too clever gentlemen think themselves bearers of the world, demi-gods... Well, let them!..."

"You can't put a horse and a trembling doe in the same cart," said Pushkin.[5] Konstantin Podovodsky apparently decided to try it in his own work, striving to combine the negative aspects of two such different poets as Balmont and Ratgauz.

Judging by the fact that on the cover of *Summit Fires* there is the label "Volume 4," one should not assume that its author is still young and searching for himself. Rather, here we have a case of innate lack of taste, contempt for the Russian language and a certain peculiar stupidity which whispers words and images to the author which are exactly the wrong ones for what his theme demands. And it is a pity! He has the temperament and poetic scope which, under favorable circumstances, might have helped him to create something of value.

Apollo, No. 6, 1910.

XIII

Poetry in *Scales*

Before 1905, when the belletristic section appeared in *Scales*, chaos reigned in Russian Symbolist poetry. Alongside Balmont and Bryusov, *World of Art*[1] promoted such dubious figures as Minsky[2]; *New Path*[3] published poems by Roslavlev, Fofanov and others. Even Skorpion, cautious Skorpion,[4] did not avoid the common fate:it published Bunin and in *Northern Flowers* printed a long poem by this same Fofanov.

Criticism hostile to the new movement in art watched all this and sniggered maliciously. Earlier cries of indignation about the "eccentricity of the Decadents" remained only in the most provincial publications, while in the more prominent ones, they were replaced either with indications that "Decadence" had been played out, or declarations that "it" never even produced anything essentially new.

Intentionally or not, I don't know, *Scales*, by including a literary section, refuted both these opinions in all its work. Thus, poems in *Scales*, especially of late, are divided into two sharply differentiated groups: the revolutionaries or the guardians of tradition. The leaders preserved for themselves the right of revolution, while the rear-guard was entrusted to the youth. Owing to this sort of formation, the whole column gained an impetus beyond that of a movement, where the leaders must simultaneously direct and restrain their forces. But this was also the reason for its disorder: one cannot and indeed should not go through the whole world like a cavalry attack...

Symbolism was dying out. The very arguments which had arisen over the definition of this apparently fully elucidated literary doctrine, indicated dissatisfaction with it in the circle of poets. New problems arose, peculiar to each master, and their works were called Symbolist only for lack of a more suitable name.

A few remarks about the poets presented in *Scales.*

Konstantin Balmont, so fragile, so incorporeal in the first period of his work, grew passionately fond of things and placed the music potentially hidden in them above everything. In his epithets he does not pursue accuracy; he wants their very sound, not the concepts hidden in them, to define the image he needs. However, even here, where possible, he changes adjectives into nouns: voiceless—voicelessness, cherishing—cherishment, etc. The last example is especially characteristic: he changed the very "cherish" into an adjective and then made a noun out of it. Neglect of verbs—that is what makes his recent poems ghastly and inert, because poetry is thought, and thought is, above all, action. Be that as it may, his endeavors are of enormous theoretical interest, and in time they will be appreciated at their true value.

Bryusov, who revived a noble art in Russia, forgotten since the time of Pushkin, writes simple and regular poems; and having given examples of classical purity and strength in *Urbi et orbi* and *Garland*,[5] like Jacob joined battle with his God. He brings assonance into poetic practice, uses hyperdactyllic rhymes, new stanzas, repetition of the same lines. Finally, in the poem "To Someone," which begins with the line "Farman or Wright, or whoever you are!"[6] he resolutely approaches the contemporaneity of which poets are so afraid, and comes out the victor.

Then come: Vyacheslav Ivanov, whose entire poetic work is a constant revolution, sometimes even against canons he established; Mikhail Kuzmin, with all the unexpected daring of his themes and devices, a vocabulary unprecedented in Russian and a verse which sounds exquisite and strange; and Andrei Bely, who attempts to bring the colorful Impressionism of his youthful works to the most everyday experiences.

Zinaida Gippius, with her mastery frozen at a single point, stands apart, as do Fyodor Sologub and Aleksandr Blok, who have printed their most characteristic poems in other publications.

Of the young poets, the "guardians of tradition," especially promoted by *Scales* are: Sergei Solovyov, Boris Sadovsky, and Viktor Gofman.

Sergei Solovyov printed his best poems in *Scales*, those in which, under the guidance of Bryusov's poetry, he continues the work of Maikov, sometimes even surpassing the latter in the chasing of the verse and the strength of its graphic quality.

Boris Soadovskoy maintains memories of the traditions of Pushkin's epoch, studying its second-rate poets. It seems that the current of Modernism has not touched him at all. However, dry precision of rhythm and image, taste and a noble striving toward work on verse reveal how close the poet is to the new trend, without which he could scarcely have freed himself from the chains of Realism, for by temperament he is no conqueror.

Viktor Gofman is a student now of Balmont, now of Bryusov. With reason, he wrote in his youth a salutory poem to both of them. But this apprenticeship did not go farther than a borrowing of devices and a similarity of images. Through a youthful admiration of the refinements of culture, his own perception of the world can be seen—a tedious but sometimes keen sensuality. And it is unfortunate that recently he has begun to imitate the seraphic Blok.

Of those more rarely published in *Scales,* one can mention Yury Verkhovsky—a poet of the Boris Sadovskoi type, but more diffuse and bookish, and Odinoky, who has set himself a series of interesting problems, and is seriously working at their solution.

One cannot say that there were not serious slips in the poetry section of *Scales;* such, for example, are its silence in regard to Innokenty Annensky (in all that time, it seems, there were no more than three notices and not one of his poems); the failure to enlist the contribution of Pyotr Potemkin, one of the most original young contemporary poets; and finally, Ellis's promotion in the last year.

But despite all these blunders, the history of *Scales* can be viewed as the history of the main course of Russian Symbolism.

Apollo, No. 8, 1910

XIV

Innokenty Annensky. *The Cypress Chest: Second Book of Poems.* (posthumous). **Grif, 1910.**
Alexander Roslavlev. *Carousels.* **SPb., 1910.**
Evgeny Kurlov. *Poems.* **Moscow, 1910.**
Alexander Rotshtein. *Sonnets.* **SPb., 1910.**
Vasily Knyazev. *Satiric Songs.* **SPb.**
Sasha Cherny. *Satires.* **SPb, 1910.**

A whole series of critical articles by Modernists, representatives of the old school and even new-comers, has appeared about Innokenty Annensky's recently published book. And it is characteristic that they all agree in judging *The Cypress Chest* an indisputably outstanding book, the creation of a great and mature talent. This was perhaps influenced by the fact that Annensky, while not siding ideologically with the circle of Russian Symbolists, nonetheless deviating significantly time and again from the goals he set himself, studied under the same teachers—the French poets, worked on the same problems, and suffered from the same doubts, although in the name of something different. The Russian Symbolists undertook a hard but noble task—to lead their national poetry out of the Babylonian bondage of ideology and prejudice in which it had languished for almost a half-century. Besides their work, they had to spread culture, to speak of basic truths, to defend passionately ideas which had already become generalities in the West. In this respect, one can compare Bryusov with Peter the Great.

Annensky remained a stranger to this battle. Whether it was the sheer estheticism of a soul spoiled by the beauties of Hellas, or a pious, although apparently egotistical striving to use his powers in the best way that forced him to isolate himself spiritually—who knows?

But only now, when poetry has won the right to be alive and develop, most of the seekers of new paths inscribe on their banner the name of Annensky as our "Tomorrow." Here is how he himself defines his relationship to Russian Symbolism in the poem entitled "To Another:"

> Your dreams are Maenades[1] by night,
> And the lunar whirlwind in the twinkling expanse
> Casts the waves of tresses up along their shoulders...
> My best dream: behind the cloth of Andromache;[2]
>
> On her head an echafaudage, [3]
> And it coquettishly covered with a kerchief,
> But nowhere would my severe pencil
> Yield a bit of its harmonies.

The last two lines are especially characteristic of our poet. In his poems he captures the harmonic balance between image and form—a balance which frees both these elements, allowing them to strive together like two brothers toward the precise embodiment of emotional experience.

The range of his ideas is sharply new and sparkles with the unexpected and sometimes the paradoxical. For him, what is typical of our era is not our faith, but our lack of it, and he fights for his right not to believe with the bitterness of a prophet. With a look burning with curiosity, he pierces the darkest, most remote recesses of the human soul; for him only pretense is odious, and the question with which he confronts the reader: "but what if filth and baseness are only torments amid the splendor somewhere shining there?"—is no longer a question for him, but an indisputable truth. *The Cypress Chest* is the catechism of contemporary sensibility.

Annensky worked long and hard on verse technique and poetic syntax and made great gains in this area. By placing the subject at the end of the sentence, he gave it a peculiar significance and power, as for example in the lines:

> I knew that she would return
> And be with me—Grief.

Whimsically reshuffling subordinate clauses, he achieved, like Mallarmé, a hieratical majesty and prompted intonations of voice unknown in poetry before him.

> Oh no, not the figure, let him be so gently vacillating,
> I from your temptations harbor
> Not the damp luster of raspberry smiles,
> But the cool serpent of suffering.

His alliterations are not accidental, the rhymes have a great power of suggestion.

The readers of *Apollo* know that Innokenty Annensky died on November 30th, 1909. And now is the time to say that not only Russia, but all of Europe, has lost one of its great poets...

Two or three years ago, when Roslavlev's[4] first book came out, Chukovsky, with his characteristic courage, stated the opinion of the educated majority, namely, that Roslavlev was a typical representative of the Modernist masses, unreliable even in a burst of enthusiasm, intoxicated with what they do not believe in and with the thoughtlessness of boors dragging the ideals of the leaders out into the street. The article caused a sensation and—what is much more important—influenced, it seems, Roslavlev himself. The mark of a certain restraint makes this new book more literary than the first. Now he is no longer dissatisfied with God, but only with human culture (the poem "Panopticum"), and borrows his ideas and images not from Artsybashev,[5] but from Leonid Andreev ("Angel"). Occasionally, amid the rehashings of almost all the Modernists, from Bryusov to Potemkin inclusive, which make up his style, there gleam his own images, and his own style begins to show through. "Uncle John" is almost all good. They say that the group of Italian "Futurist" artists vowed not to draw "nu" for ten years, so that this genre of painting would once again regain its original freshness. If Roslavlev would renounce the fatal idea of deciding universal questions with home remedies, drawing his knowledge of philosophy from Balmont's poems, if he would stop speaking in generalities about the City and the Devil, if he would try to develop his taste, then he would be a poet.

Evgeny Kurlov obviously intends to imitate Sologub. This is apparent both in the pretentious introduction (a sort of manifesto of extreme individualism) and in the predominance of lyrical reflection over images and colors in his book. Sometimes this leads to good results; you find true streaks in the book, singing lines, no banal ideas. But alas, the exacting style of Sologub is not within Kurlov's power, and he often makes use of words and ideas from a more accessible poet—Balmont. And this creates an unpleasant impression, because the time for imitating Balmont has already passed, and the time for studying him has not yet come.

According to the advertisement in the collection in question, it seems that Kurlov has already published three books.[6] It is sad to think that one must explain the wretched cries, the comic inaccuracies that mottle his poems not by the early youth of the author, but by something else.

Love of the sonnet usually flares up either in a period of poetic renaissance, or on the contrary, in a period of decline. In the first case, one finds new possibilities in the tight sonnet form: either the meter varies, or the rhyme alternations change; in the second case, one seeks out the most complicated and inflexible and at the same time most typical formula for the sonnet, and it takes on the character of a canon. The sonnets of Shakespeare and the sonnets of Hérédia,[7] these are the two poles in the history of the sonnet, and both are irreproachable. The difference in their reception especially allows one to evaluate their charm, as always in sonnets based exclusively on inspired calculation. In both, the refinement of effect goes hand in hand with confidence of expression and lapidarity of style.

After this short *aperçu*, what can one say about the sonnets of Alexander Rotshtein?[8] The exacting sonnetist would not have written sonnets in anapests or with only masculine rhymes, would not have rhymed four adjectives or three verbal adverbs in a row, would not have repeated the very same line twice. . . But the daring innovator would have found the necessary words, instead of the cliches of cheap estheticism, which is what all the ideas and images in Alexander Rotshtein's book come to.

For me, it is beyond doubt that for a good satirist, a certain bluntness of perception and narrowness of horizon are indispensable, that is, what is generally called common sense. It is well known that people of the higher sort, ennobled through long poetic contemplation, do not laugh and do not become indignant. Such, according to Marcel Schwob,[9] was Whitman.

But perhaps we love satire because it is the voice of the crowd, trying to state its opinion of life, of the world, of everything about which usually only the elect speak. And there is nothing surprising in the fact that, not having learned to revere, it only despises, but in such a way that its disdain is sometimes worth a great deal of reverence.

I do not know why, of the two elements of satire, disdain and indignation, Vasily Knyazev[10] chose the latter. Not having the great talent of a Nekrasov or even the inventiveness of a Minaev,[11] he is forced to content himself with meaningless phrases like the traditional "punishing lash," "mournful songs," "poor sufferer of the people," and so forth (everything listed was copied from one page). He roundly abuses Otto Weininger[12] (whom, as is clear from the poem, he has either not read or not understood), abuses contemporary writers for their immorality and many others who happened to attract his attention. His verse, not without a certain pleasant glibness, and is almost always unoriginal and resembles now Kurochkin,[13] now Minaev, now Veinberg.[14] But it seems to me that he does have talent.

Sasha Cherny chose the better part—disdain. But he has enough taste to occasionally replace his peevish smile with a gracious or even good-natured one. He is very observant and searches not for people's vices, like Knyazev, but their characteristic traits, so that it is not always his fault if they only turn out to be ridiculous. He loves nature shyly but passionaltely, and he becomes a real poet when speaking of her. Besides that, he even has his own philosophy—a consistent pessimism which does not spare the author himself. His verse, original and cultivated, abounds with the intonations of the spoken language, and even his awkwardness makes you happy, as a promise of the poet's future development of himself. But even now his *Satires* are a valuable contribution to our poor satiric literature.

XV

Fyodor Sologub. *Collected Works.* Vols. 1,5. Spb.: Shipovnik.
Sergei Solovyov. *April: Second Book of Poems.* Moscow: Musaget,
1910.
Nikolai Morzov. *Star Songs.* Moscow: Skorpion, 1910.
Nikolai Brandt. *No Peace for My World: Poems.* Kiev, 1910.
Sergei Gedroits. *Verse and Tales.* SPb., 1910.

Sologub has written a great deal, but there may be even more
written about him. So perhaps it is unnecessary labor to write
about him again. But when I read critiques of Sologub, strange
questions crop up, so simply formulated as to be inappropriate.
How can this be so? He is Gogol's successor but has not established any particular school; he is a refined stylist, but the majority of his poems are almost indistinguishable from one another;
he is a formidable visionary, but of his visions we only remember
Nedotykomka, the Dog and the star Mair.[1] Why this happens I
do not know and will not attempt to give an answer, but I will
try to examine the poetry of Sologub from the point of view of
the general demands made of the poet.

Sologub's images...but what kind of images can there be if
the poet has said there is only "self," which is the sole reality,
and which created the world. And it is not surprising that this
world is only a desert in which there is nothing to love, because
love means to feel something higher and better than yourself, and
this is impossible by definition. As if through a glass blackened
with soot, the poet looks about him. There are no colors, and
lines too are somewhow suspiciously obliterated; the light of dawn
through it is cold and sad, life—pale, the day—clear, the abyss—
mute. His vocabulary is noble, but so inexpressive; compare it
even with the vocabulary of Bryusov or Balmont; not to mention
Ivanov or Annensky, in whom the adjective, by its depth and color,
completely overwhelms the noun.

The reluctance to sketch and model is especially telling in
Sologub's rhymes; for rhyme in verse is the same as the angle in
the plastic arts: the transition from one line to another must be
outwardly unexpected, inwardly substantiated, free, delicate
and resilient. But Sologub, rhyming identical forms of verbs or
adjectives, taking the endings of such words as *gadaniia, veshcha-
niia* for dactylic rhymes, unwittingly de-wings his verse.

The strength of Sologub as a poet lies in the fact that he has been and has remained the only consistent Decadent. Everything that wounds a sick consciousness is removed from his poems; his images are minute and disappear, leaving behind a scarcely audible melody, perhaps only an aroma. To achieve this, he does not depict things as he sees them, and loves most of all "what is not in the world." His muse is "the angel of dreams unseen on paths untrod," who, as on a knightly shield with a coat of arms, holds in her hands "an unread book, with a forbidden secret." And of course, he speaks most of all about death, this great poet-mystifier who obviously never died, although he loved to affirm the contrary.

Poets have various inspirations: the inspiration of love, of suffering, of wisdom, of power. Sergei Solovyov chose for himself the inspiration of well-being. Speaking of Kiev he exclaims:

> Was it not here that the Byzantine sovereigns
> Sent their precious gifts?
> In the chambers the cries did not fall silent,
> Nor the loud and heady feats.

Here, about Russia:

> All of Russia is grain and sky.
> Hundreds of miles—all the same:
> Golden waves of grain,
> Rye swelling with the wind

Here, about the estates of Lord Ravenswood:[2]

> Not one forbidden, ancient fir
> In the wood did the enemy axe touch,
> And far away in the markets, the trout
> From your deep lakes is famous.

Here, about ancient Greece:

> Dirty with earth and golden dung,
> With strong hands, like white bark,
> You squeeze the nipples of a stubborn wild goat,
> And streams of milk ring against the bottom of the pail.

He loves books, the old ones more—not to read them, however, but to admire them in some small but select library or to take one along with him to the woods, to somehow justify his dreamy wanderings. Obviously, he is not a reader, because all of his bookish images—Joan of Arc, and Richard the Lion-Hearted, and John the Baptist—are only feeble re-tellings of events famous in history and legend.

As a true man of the soil, he is sensual. All the naive eroticism of the eighteenth century, with its "beauties not more than fourteen," "Bosoms," and other "hidden charms" occupied a not unimportant place in his poems. But where a more serious attitude toward love appears, he is almost a student of Apukhtin.[3]

It is wonderful to see in him a real closeness to Byzantium. For it is through Byzantium that we Russians inherit the beauty of *Hellas,* as the French inherit it through Rome. And often Greek idylls and elegies, played out on lawns in suburban Moscow, are the personal achievements of the poet Sergei Solovyov, and have their own special keenness.

Compared with Sergei Solovyov's first book, his verse is improving, but rather along the lines of delicacy and melodiousness than of forged brass, as the poet himself dreams. The only thing that is annoying is the sometimes careless attitude toward the Russian language. Such expressions as "oral roses," "the faun panpipes into the melodious trunk," "sweet-grassed verdure of the earth"—all this is simply misunderstood by Vyacheslav Ivanov.

Boom, boom, boom!
Bo-bo-boom!
Who thunders
In the hills?
It is god
Boomboomgod.
He eats beans and peas!
O, you god!
Boomboomgod!
Don't you eat
All the peas!
To your feast,
Commander,
Invite the whole world!

What is it? A parody on Ivan Rukavishnikov? No, it is a poem by Nikolai Morozov.[4] This is his humor. But here are some serious lines:

He sought the long path to the truth
In the vale of lies and vulgarities.

A deep blackness shrouded him,
And no light from heaven burned.
etc.

Here are some especially starry ones:

In the skyblue hemisphere,
There, where the Milky Way glitters,
Appeared in the atmosphere
Above the earth a meteorite.
etc.

Is it possible that an author along in years can make his debut with a book of poems which have such a collection of images, devices and crystallized experiences? Or is it that scientific poetry that René Ghil[5] and his supporters are talking about so much in France? No, there, everything is based on the search for a synthesis between art and science, but in Nikolai Morozov's poems, we see neither. Only magnificent contempt for style, mockery of the demands of taste and a complete failure to understand the purpose of verse, so characteristic of the Russian poet-revolutionaries of the end of the nineteenth century, and perhaps also banality of experience, dullness of poetic perception and rudeness in regard to eternal themes—that is Morozov's poetry.

Why did you visit us
In the backwoods of a forgotten village?... [6]

The major distinguishing trait of Nikolai Brandt's[7] poems is their prosiness. When the idea or image is prosaic, you can still accept the situation: the author, it seems, is sufficiently intelligent and well-read not to try to mask this shortcoming, characteristic of many greater poets, but the prosaism of his expressions is often too agonizing: he tempts you so to slam that little book shut so

73

that you will not ever open it again. As if aware of this, Nikolai Brandt sometimes falls into the opposite extreme, and writes things that have the taste not even of sugar, but of saccharine. Such is his "epic in symbols," "Through Life."

His themes are banal-decadent with an inclination towards Parnassianism, from which, by the way, this poet, almost unsurpassed in the amusing clumsiness of his expressions, is still so far removed: The Curse of Eve, The Alexandrian Executioner, The Dance of Solume, Dream of a Masochist, Mandragora,[8] The Sorrow of Satan, etc.

But good lines do turn up in his work, sometimes even good stanzas. Here, for example, is the beginning of the poem "The Labor of Sysiphus:"

> Wedging his foot in the sand, clenching his teeth until they hurt,
> Straining the iron knots of muscle,
> The shaggy giant, pushing the rough rock,
> Tries to roll it to the summit of the cliff.

It is amusing to note that the title of the book is printed in the shape of a cup. Apparently even Ivan Rukavishnikov, who has written several "figured poems," has not only admirers, but even imitators.

Why do poets write? It is not difficult to answer this question: some—to tell people something new that happened to them personally: an idea, an image, a feeling, it does not matter; others, for the pure delight of creation, divinely complex, joyously difficult. But why do non-poets write; why, for example, does Sergei Gedroits?[9]

It is not "the chafing of a captive thought," because there are no thoughts in his poems, there are only generalities; vanity? hardly; he only with difficulty imitates poor imitators of Apukhtin. Why then? Why?

His style is terrible; Vladimir Gordin himself does not have a style like this:

> Falling asleep from thoughts of inconsolable anguish,
> I whispered your name yesterday.
> And you came to me from the unknown distances,
> From the transparent dome of the height of the heavens
> You descended, as soon as I summoned you.

74

Falling asleep from thoughts of anguish, "tvóe" (instead of "tvoë"), "dalí" (instead of "dáli"), dome of the height of the heavens—is all that really Russian? And it is the same on every page. Everything is accidental in this book, unstable and viscous like a boggy swamp: you can exchange one adjective for another, rearrange the stanzas, make one poem out of several and several out of one.

There are even pictures in the book, just as unnecessary and colorless as the poems.

Apollo, No. 9, 1910.

XVI

Ivan Bunin. *Complete Works,* Vol. VI. SPb., 1910.
Yury Sidorov. *Poems.* Moscow: Altsiona, 1910.[1]
Yury Verkhovsky. *Idylls and Elegies.* SPb.: Ory.
Negin. *The Coming Faust.* Riazan, 1910.

Poetry should hypnotize—in this lies its strength. But the methods of this hypnotism are different, they depend on the conditions in each country and epoch. Thus, in the beginning of the nineteenth century, when, with the memory of revolution still fresh, France strove toward the ideal of a government of the common man, French poetry leaned toward antiquity as the cultural basis of all civilized peoples. Germany, dreaming of union, resurrected native folklore. England, having paid tribute to self-adoration in the persons of Coleridge and Wordsworth, found expression for her society's temperament in the heroic poetry of Byron.

Later Hugo hypnotized with his affectation, so unusual for facile French poetry after the eighteenth century. Heine hypnotized with his sarcasm, the Parnassians, with exoticism, Pushkin and Lermontov with new possibilities for the Russian language.

And when the most intense moment in the life of our nation had passed, and everything more or less leveled off, the Symbolists came onto the field, wishing to hypnotize not with themes, but with the very method of their communication. They wore out one's attention, first with original suggestive repetitions (Edgar Allen Poe), then with intentional obfuscation of the basic theme

(Mallarmé), then with flashing images (Balmont), then with archaic words and expressions (Vyacheslav Ivanov), and attaining this, suggested the appropriate feeling.

Symbolist art will predominate until the fermentation of contemporary thought ceases, or—on the contrary—becomes so strong that one can harmonize it poetically. This is why one must consider Bunin's poetry, and that of other imitators of Naturalism, as mere counterfeits, most of all because they are dull and do not hypnotize. Everything in them is clear, and nothing is beautiful.

When you read Bunin's poetry, it seems that you are reading prose. The apt details of landscape are not interconnected by a lyrical development. The thoughts are niggardly and rarely go beyond a simple trick. Great flaws turn up in both the verse and the Russian. And if you try to reconstruct the spiritual side of Bunin from his poems, the picture turns out even sadder: reluctance or inability to delve deep inside himself, a dreaminess that is uninspired in the absence of fantasy, a keenness of observation without enthusiasm for the thing observed, and an absence of the temperament that alone makes a man a poet.

Yury Sidorov, who died about a year and a half ago, was what is called an interesting man, to judge by the article-obituaries by Andrei Bely, Sergei Solovyov and Boris Sadovskoi which are appended to his book of poems. You can believe that when reading his poetry, still so immature, so imitative. Rarely, but sometimes at least, his own themes appear, for example, the poem "Oleograph"; the basic columns of the poetic structure he conceived already begin to take shape: the England of Sir Walter Scott, the mysticism of Egypt and a hidden passion for Byzantium. His love of the eighteenth century seems accidental to me, and too clearly inspired by Kuzmin.

Certainly one ought to reproach the poet for his imitation of the writing manner of the poets from Pushkin's time, which leads him finally to an imitation of Benediktov;[2] and for his imitation of the contemporary "wizard," which makes him write, for example, such lines as these:

> Palace of Yaldabaoth[3]
> Faded with the gall of angry days,
> Through you we with knowledge became gods,
> O promised, prophetic serpent.

It is possible to analyze this, but it is boring. It seems time to leave Yaldabaoth to the popularizers of religious history.

Idylls and Elegies by Yury Verkhovsky[4] is a better example of how much one can do in poetry, without even possessing great talent. This book will become the friend of everyone who simply loves poetry, not searching in it for something to arouse dulled nerves, for new horizons, or for answers to world problems. In Yury Verkhovsky's poetry there is no daring, but at the same time there is no outcry, clumsiness or annoying carelessness of form. Many poems are good, and there is not one bad one. The poet consciously chose for himself the role of Theon. Remember in Zhukovsky:[5]

> ...Theon, near domestic Penates,
> Modest in his desires, without splendid hopes,
> Stayed on the shore of Alphea.[6]

And he did not miscalculate. In his verse is everything nature can give a simple, untroubled soul—the joy of the morning, the quiet pleasure of the day and all the intimacy of evening, and at night—dreams of reminiscences whose traces no one can find. His landscapes are not as clear as Bunin's, but much more delicate and fresh, as befits landscapes of the north.

And on all of his poems lies the mark of his perception's distinctive feature, which the poet himself depicts best of all:

> Visions of earth
> Flooded with radiance;
> And shrouds of simplicity
> Envelop the sky.

In this book, Yury Verkhovsky is already a fully developed poet, who, if he is to study, then only under such masters as Pushkin, Baratynsky and Delvig.

The Coming Faust by Mr. Negin[7] could only appear in Russia. He clearly disapproves of all the starry-eyed conversations about ancient Russian culture, and our capacity for quickly seizing ideas from the West. In the book there is not one even slightly unfeigned line, not one even slightly uncommonplace thought. The verse is exceptionally bad. However, it seems that it was not a "poet" who worked out this book, but an advocate of social reconstruction, partly in the spirit of Lev Tolstoi. He made use of the dramatic form as a means of popularizing his ideas, with the same touching ingenuousness as earlier writers of geography in verse.

Apollo, No. 10, 1910.

XVII

Modest Druzhinin. —K.E. Antonov. *Blissful Distances.* —Baron N. A. Vrangel. —Vladimir Gessen. *Yellow Leaves.* —Sergei Alyakrinsky. *Chains of Fire.* —Alexander Mitrofanovich Fedorov. —Dmitry Svyatopolk-Mirsky. *Poems.* —E. Astori. *Dissonances.* E. I. Shtein. —Sofia Dubnova. *Autumn Pipe.* —Igor Severyanin. —Fyodor Kashintsev. *Pains of the Heart.* —F. Lado-Svetogorsky. —Sergei Klychkov. *Songs.* —Modest Gofman. *Hymns and Odes.* —Velimir Khlebnikov, Vladimir Kamensky. *Hatchery of Judges.* —Ellis. *Stigmata.* —Benedikt Livshits. *The Flute of Marsyas.* —Marina Tsvetaeva. *Evening Album.* —Ilya Ehrenburg.

1

Before me I have twenty books of poems, almost all by young or at very least unknown poets. Strictly speaking, only four stand outside literature, however wide the meaning of that ill-fated word. Three are Modest Druzhinin's,[1] completely lacking not only poetic temperament and knowledge of the technique of poetic creation, but even an elementary feeling of irony, which allows him to address his beloved with this sort of "Entreaty":

> Why should you guard your innocence,
> Vainly torment yourself with passion,—
> Pay tribute to nature, pay that debt
> And let me possess you!

And one is K. E. Antonov's *Blissful Distances.*[2] He simply did not learn how and when one can use "high-class" words. Expressions like "the worshipper of terrible depravity," "conceives an opinion of himself," etc. mottle his badly rhymed lines.

78

The other books I would like to divide into amateurish ones, daring ones, and books by writers.

Let us begin with the first group. For my life, I would not be able to understand why they appear, if the authors themselves had not obligingly explained in verse or prose. Thus, one of them, paying his inability to write its due, and declining all praise in advance, hopes to touch certain of his female acquaintances with his poems.

Another informs us that in publishing, he is fulfilling the will of his wife, who has died. A third justifies himself by the fact that he first thought "of illustrating a musical work with poems" (I do not know how successful this idea was). And more in the same vein.

Not all the collections of this type are invariably awful. For example, Vladimir Gessen's *Yellow Leaves*[3] is almost good. It contains poems from 1889-1892, and indeed, if they had been printed in good time, they would have given the author an honorable position among the representatives of Russian poetry of the time! His verse is perhaps too facile, confident and melodious, the thoughts and images, although worn thin (now), reveal good taste. For the dilettante reader or the anemic, who find the poetry of recent years, complicated and rich in its internal content, slightly beyond their powers, this book can provide a real pleasure.

Unfortunately one cannot say the same about the poems of Baron N. A. Vrangel.[4] The book is dated 1911, but there is not even a shadow of that delicacy, that instinctive knowledge of the laws of poetry in it, that there is in Vladimir Gessen's poems, which are close to these in method and direction. The author is for some reason captive of a pose that was the mode about thirty years ago—that of the champion of an ideal, coldly pious, affectedly sincere, coolly and listlessly enamoured of his love, tearfully enraptured with his homeland, and wildly ecstatic with Italy. It is obvious that he is not at all interested in the fate of poetry, and perhaps does not even guess that such a thing exists; for him there are no ideals in the future, no precious memories in the past. I do not believe that he has read Pushkin.

No better, although in a completely different vein, is Sergei Alyakrinsky, who wrote the book *Chains of Fire*.[5] He is a Modernist: when you find a sloppy rhyme in his work, he will tell you it is assonance; if you ask him about some line for which there is no place in the metrical scheme, however contrived it may be, he will declare that its rhythm caresses his ear; if you express bewilderment in regard to the expression "the emanating calls of the day," he will turn his back on you. The timid reader really has reason to be disconcerted. But leaf through his book, and you will be reassured. He has no understanding of assonance, he is completely innocent of rhythmic innovations, his soul is no more refined by his emotional experiences than your own, he is the typical dilettante, except that he writes not like Nadson, but like Balmont and Blok. He developed the most questionable features of the talents of these two poets, he obscured their obscure expressions, screamed in those passages where they raised their voice, and tried to scare us. They won't understand me, he thought, but then, they didn't understand Bryusov at first either. And he can always find himself a critic who is not educated enough to study more complicated phenomena, who will declare him the only real poet, among so many versifiers, who brings to the world the "message of Spring."

Then for a whole season he will shine in the editorial offices as a young talent. Such things have happened and do happen. However, I hope that this will not happen to him. He shows too little enthusiasm in his filibusterous attack upon Russian literature.

Gessen, Baron Vrangel and Alyakrinsky are models of the three categories of poet-dilettantes.

Here are several varieties: Alexander Mitrofanovich Fedorov[6] wields verse better than Gessen, and is perhaps more "trained," but he creates the impression of a sort of eunuch in poetry. His high notes quite often turn shrill, and he perceives the world not even like a woman, but just like an old lady, a eunuch, a world which for him is either "a vale of grief and sorrow," or "a soundless prayer," or simply falls apart into a series of details unconnected by a general progression. And the author's declarations that his soul is akin... to Imatra[7] Falls, do not destroy, but support this opinion. However, the poems where he imitates Bunin are sometimes quite literary.

More refined, newer, but still in the same vein are the *Poems* of Prince Dmitry Svyatopolk-Mirsky.[8] Reading them, one wonders if the author did not purposely narrow his horizon, reject sharp emotional experiences and exciting images, grow fond of the most unexpressive epithets, so that nothing would distract one's thought from the smooth succession of fine and sonorous stanzas. It is as if he is still afraid to admit he is a poet, and until he does, I do not wish to be more bold than he.

I would say that E. Astori, who published the book *Dissonances*,[9] has a secret affinity of soul with Baron N.A. Vrangel, if their souls were even the slightest bit involved in the creation of their poems.

E. I. Shtein's book,[10] which is entirely filibusterous, has an unexpected vagary. The author does not imitate anyone, but wants to express only one sensation, namely, surprise at the most commonplace phenomena. He does this, it is true, with only the aid of exclamation points, and the inopportunely placed pronoun "such," and for this reason is not in any position to contaminate the reader. But the attempt to create from the book a sort of proclamation of a new (in this case not terribly new) attitude is interesting in itself. I would not have thought of placing him in the category of the daring if his poems more closely resembled poems. But now it seems that he landed in literature completely by accident.

The author of the book *Autumn Pipe*, Sofia Dubnova,[11] is completely under the spell of Blok. She is indebted to him for her images, emotional experiences, rhymes, rhythms and so forth. The original is good and the copy is not at all as bad as some critics thought. But it is a dangerous path. To surpass Blok in his own field, one needs a quite exceptional talent, but Sofia Dubnova did not project her paths of development.

The reader is perhaps surprised that I devoted so much space to the poems of "amateurs." But young writers must dissociate themselves from those whom they wrongly consider or could consider their confederates. For it is just as unfair to see in Emelyanov-Kokhanovsky[12] one of the founders of Russian Symbolism, as it is to see in Alyakrinsky and poets of his kind the successors of Blok and Bely.

2

Sometime, about twenty years ago, there were very few daring poets, and they were worth their weight in gold. And indeed, when war was declared on the past, when we had to rush to the assault, what could have been more useful than cannon fodder? Through the debris of hysteria and posing the young contemporary poets came to the shrine of art. But I do not think that this path was profitable for the new seekers after "their own." The young contemporary poets are no longer Chekhovian heroes striving to escape from a stuffy life, but seafarers like Sinbad, deserting blessed Bagdad "to look curiously at new subjects." And only a reverent attitude toward the greatest wealth of poets, toward their native language, saves them, as Sinbad was saved by reverence for the laws of Allah.

Of all the daring poets whose books now lie before me, the most interesting is perhaps Igor Severyanin: he is more daring than all the rest. Of course, it is impossible to take nine-tenths of his work as anything more than a desire for scandal, or as incomparably pitiful naivete. Where he wants to be elegant, he resembles a parody on the novels of Anastasia Verbitskaya, he is clumsy when he wants to be refined, his daring is not always far from insolence. "I am branded as Baudelaire once was," "well-parted... a cavalier desirable to many," "Menshevik," "grisette," and similar expressions only hint at all the clumsiness of his style. However, his verse is free and inspired, his images truly and sometimes happily unexpected, he already has his poetic persona. I will quote one poem, which shows his keen fantasy, his inclination toward irony and a certain cold intimacy.

South in the North

I left by the eskimo hut
A skewbald reindeer,—he looked at me wisely,
   And I got fruit
   And started drinking wine.
And in the tundra—you understand?—it was southerly...
In the cracks of ice—the click of castanets...
   And I burst out laughing a pearl laugh,
   Training my lorgnette upon the eskimo!

It is difficult, and I do not wish to judge now whether this is good or bad. It is new—thank you for that.

The joyless daring of Fyodor Kashintsev in his book *Pains of the Heart*[15] is not promising. He speaks of the loathsomeness of life and the horror of death, of the eternal lie and universal decay, perhaps with the grimace of Prometheus but not thunderously, only whiningly. He gives too little basis for justification of his pessimism, and he expresses it in words that are too colorless, bare of metaphors. The few beautiful lines and stanzas drown in this book that always repeats the same things about the same thing. No, a philosophical lyric is not written that way. Baratynsky and Tyutchev could show Fyodor Kashintsev a great deal, if he plans to continue writing poetry.

The next three books show peculiar daring: Lado-Svetogorsky, Sergei Klychkov and Modest Gofman. All three try to squeeze their work into a narrow framework—the first—into the framework of a single definite image, the other two—of a definite style. Such a Procrustean bed can scarcely be termed desirable in poetry, although it does save us, as an outward discipline, from many *gaffes* which might be made without it.

F. Lado-Svetogorsky speaks of the Azure Country,[16] of that paradise everyone envisions. He even tries to outline its topography, gives names to its valleys and rivers. But his words are so dead, there is so little of the sharpness of a real hallucination in his descriptions, that we see only a dream, and not sensation, hope and not faith. Such a book commits neither the author nor the reader to anything.

In Sergei Klychkov's *Songs*[17] it is difficult to tell what belongs to the poet himself, and what to Balmont and Gorodetsky. It seems that he only stumbled accidentally upon the theme of heathen Russia, and started working on it too hurriedly; there is neither Russian daring, Russian sorrow, nor that strange crossing of Byzantine, Finnish, magic and Indian culture in which atmosphere Russia was born—only a confection, a Slavic Arcadia with its unfailing Ladas and Lelyas, princesses and maidens. The rhythmic refinements, the abundance of assonance, so valued in Russian songs, are replaced in his book by metrically plain lines and dull rhymes. It is just like an explanatory text for the paintings of Mrs. Böhm.[18] The advertisement on the cover promises a second book of verse by the same author—*Dubravna* and an epic "The Lament of Jaroslavna." If Sergei Klychkov does not try to widen his poetic horizon as soon as possible, he is on a dangerous path.

Modest Gofman wrote the very elegantly printed book *Hymns and Odes.*[19] From some newspaper I learned that this book was written under the influence of the author's trip to Greece.

This explains and excuses a great deal: its deliberate non-contemporaneity, the wide use of effects that have ceased to be such for us, the poverty of poetic devices, the mistakes in Russian; but it especially emphasizes other shortcomings: diffuseness of thought, insipid images and absolutely inexcusable carelessness in translation. Thus, in the Homeric hymn to Dionysus, the poet asks God, who fertilized the vineyards, for long life, but in Modest Gofman's translation—he asks for a happy, carefree youth; in the hymn to Hera, Homer says that the gods honor her as an equal of Zeus; Modest Gofman translates: "Gods... honor with the lightning-bearing Zeus to the Goddess bring." It seems to me that the reason for such distortions of the original is the translator's insufficient ability to deal with the difficulties of Russian verse.

The whole book is written in rare antique meters, which, although this is not the first time they appear in Russian poetry, still, taken together, are a pleasant novely for the general public.

The height of daring this year, of course, is the collection *Hatchery of Judges,*[20] printed on the back of wallpaper, without the letter "b," without hard signs and with some other tricks too. Of the five poets who submitted poems to it, only two are really daring: Vasily Kamensky and Velimir Khlebnikov; the rest are simply impotent.

Vasily Kamensky speaks of Russian nature. It is boundless for him, so he can comprehend only details. The relation of large branches to small ones, the cry of the cuckoo in the forest, the play of small fish under a raft—these are the themes of his poems, and it is good, because the poet does not have to strain his voice, and everything he says comes out naturally. Even his countless neologisms, sometimes very daring, the reader understands without difficulty, and from the whole cycle of poems, carries away the impression of fresh and happy novelty.

Velimir Khlebnikov is a visionary. His images are convincing in their absurdity, his ideas, in their paradoxicality. It seems that he dreams his poems and later writes them down, preserving all the incoherence of the series of events. In this respect, one can compare him with Aleksei Remizov,[21] who used to write his dreams. But Remizov is a theoretician, he simplifies the contours, outlines

84

them with a thick black border, to emphasize the significance of "dream" logic. Velimir Khlebnikov preserves all the nuances, so that his verse, losing in literariness, gains in depth. This sometimes results in completely incomprehensible neologisms, far-fetched rhymes, turns of speech that offend the most accommodating taste. But then, what doesn't one dream, and in dreams everything is significant and valuable in itself.

Among the poets daring in conception, one can count the author of *Stigmata*, Ellis, as well. He knows how verse should be written, skillfully, although somewhat monotonously, combines idea with image, and uses beautiful verse worked out, in the main, by Bryusov. But here is his task: "In all its triple consistency, the book *Stigmata...* is a symbolic representation of the whole mystical path." And for verse-representation, verse-means of expression, there is insufficient internal self-justification, joyful enthusiasm and development of the verse-end-in-itself. Perhaps Mr. Ellis could write a beautiful book of meditations and descriptions of his mystical path, really experienced and valuable, but why this should be in verse, I do not know.

Flute of Marsya,[22] a book by Benedict Livshitz, sets itself serious, and most importantly, purely literary tasks, and handles them, perhaps not always skillfully, but at least with inspiration. Its themes are often non-artistic, and forced as well: the sinful love of some girls for Christ (there are things toward which, even for esthetic considerations, one should act reverently), the rational apotheosis of sterility, etc. Such non-contagion of the poet with his themes is reflected in the epithets, monochrome-bright, as if discovered by electric light. But then, the supple, dry, confident verse, the deep and apt metaphors, the ability to let others feel an actual emotional experience in every poem, —all of this places the book in the truly valuable class and makes it not only a promise but an achievement. In the book, there are in all twenty-five poems, but it is apparent that they are the fruit of long preparation. And you believe not that this is a lethargy of creative spirit, but rather the laconicism of ambitious youth aspiring to greatness.

Marina Tsvetaeva in the book *Evening Album* is inwardly talented, and inwardly original. Although it is true that her book is dedicated to "the memory of the splendid Maria Bashkirtseva,"[23] and the epigraph taken from Rostand, the word "mama" is almost never off the page. All this only suggests the youth of the poetess, which is confirmed by her own verse-confessions. Much is new in this book: new is the (sometimes excessively) daring intimacy; new are the themes, for example childhood love; new is the spontaneous, unthinking admiration for the trifles of life. And, as one would have thought, here all the most important laws of poetry are instinctively divined, so that this book is not just a charming book of girlish confessions, but a book of fine poetry.

Ilya Ehrenburg set himself a series of interesting tasks: to re-real the visage of a medieval knight, who has only accidentally turned up in our surroundings, to portray the Catholic love for the Virgin Mary, to be refined, to create clear, expressive verse. Not one of these tasks did he even remotely fulfill, having none of the essential qualities. Here is his feeling for the Middle Ages: "...the king, surrounded by vassals, carelessly sets right the crown." Here is an appeal to the Virgin Mary: "Recall how in sinful languor you hid sinful thoughts. And in a cave on harsh straw to your shame bore the Son." Here are "refined" images: "You ran to the garden after white flowers," or "on the thin [?] little table was hot chocolate tenderly [?] served in little lilac cups," or "and you lazily moved the pink vessel, to give a special shine to your delicate nails." But to create any sort of verse, he must write *"lili"* instead of *"lilii,"* *"pàzhi"* instead of *"pazhi,"* and Mary, in his poem, longs "after her cavaliers."

Apollo, Nos. 4 and 5, 1911.

XVIII

Vladimir Kulchinsky. *The Broken Harp.* Yaroslavl, 1910.
Konstantin Bolshakov. *Mosaic: Poetry and Prose.* 1911
Vladimir Narbut. *Poems.* Book I. SPb., 1910.
Alexander Diesperov. *Poems.* Moscow, 1911.
Lev Zilov. *Poems.* Book II. Moscow, 1911.

For the critic who wishes to be conclusive and, if possible, useful to his readers as well, it would follow that he must adhere to many "working hypotheses." One of them is especially handy:

that is the division of writers by their creative quality into the categories of the competent, gifted and talented.

There are many competent ones, very many. They rarely end up in the journals, but read their verses in drawing-rooms, leaving the impression of some sort of peculiar emptiness, and they say that they do not want to publish and write for themselves. But once they have come out with a book, they usually become more unpleasant and speak of jealousy and writers' intrigues.

The gifted fill up the empty pages of journals with their works, appear at philanthropic soirées and among their acquaintances (who sometimes include critics) are considered promising young poets, although they are already over forty. Of the talented it is not worth speaking: they are always individual and each deserves special analysis.

Vladimir Kulchinsky is hardly even competent: he is simply lethargic. In his lethargy he makes use of the most hackneyed ideas, feelings and images; having started to sketch some picture, he never carries it through, he has never had the desire to use a new rhyme, a new meter. His book is a contemporary *Telemachiad*:[1] it too one can force people to read as a form of punishment.

It seems to me that only inexperience and inability to treat his works critically prevents Konstantin Bolshakov, author of the book *Mosaic*[2] from moving from the category of the competent to that of the gifted. Only the first verses are positively awful; all these little bladelets of grass and breezelets, reminiscences and day-dreams reek of painful boredom. But then the later ones, imitations of Balmont, though sometimes a bit too servile, gladden with their genuine spontaneity and a certain peculiar, youthful exaltation. The prose passages in the book are worse than weak.

Diesperov is gifted. He worked on *The Golden Fleece*[4] and, it seems, on *The Pass,*[5] 'and "Grif"[6] published his book. In every poem there is something which justifies its existence—a thought, a feeling.... But both these thoughts and these feelings are just as meager as the rhythms and words. Diesperov's poetry is like a model for real poetry: everything is there, everything is in place, but everything is 1/10 its real size. Too much effort is necessary on the part of the reader for his images to become live, the colors sparkling. Will everyone want to crack a coconut shell to get a sunflower seed? Diesperov is a private without hope of ever becoming a general.

Narbut's book of poems[7] does not produce a bad impression: in contrast to Diesperov's book, it is brilliant. There are technical devices in it that charm the reader (although there are also some which cool his ardor), there are apt descriptions (although there are artificial ones too), there is intimacy (sometimes affectation as well). But how can one not forgive failures in the presence of successes? A good impression—but why does this book awaken wistful reflections? It contains nothing besides pictures of nature: of course even in these one can express one's world view, one's individual sorrow and individual joy, everything that is valuable in poetry—but this is exactly what Narbut failed to do. Why is this? Has the poet really ceased to be a microcosm? Has the time of vulgar specialization by theme really come for poetry as well? Or is this only the distinctive device of a strong talent, developing its abilities one at a time? I hope to God! In that case it is dreadful only for him, and not for all of poetry.

There is no better way to poison one's faith in young poets, perhaps even in young poetry, than to read through the "poems" of Lev Zilov.[8] Everything, thoughts and devices, are taken from one man...Boris Zaitsev.[9] Let it not be said in reproach to the latter that what is good in prose is unbearably tedious in poetry. And in general, what sort of tastelessness is this—for a poet to imitate a prose-writer! Every thought conditions its form in advance—poetic, prosaic, pictorial or musical, otherwise it is not a thought, but thoughtlessness.

Apollo, No. 6, 1911.

XIX

1

Vyacheslav Ivanov. *Cor Ardens.* **Part One. Moscow: Skorpion, 1911. 2 R. 40 k.**

If it is true—and it is most likely—that the poet *is* the blazingly creative feat of his life, that poetry *is* the truthful narration of the genuinely experienced mystical path, that Confucious, Mohammed, Socrates and Nietzsche are poets, then Vyacheslav Ivanov is a poet too. An immeasurable gulf separates him from the poets of line and color, Pushkin or Bryusov, Lermontov or Blok. Their poetry is a lake which reflects the sky, the poetry of Vyacheslav Ivanov is the sky reflected in a lake. Their heroes, their landscapes are more lofty as they become more lifelike; the perfection of Vyacheslav Ivanov's images depends on their illusory quality. The Lermontovian Demon descends from the heights of perfect knowledge to Georgia to kiss the eyes of a beautiful girl; the hero of Vyacheslav Ivanov's epic, black-legged Melamp, goes off to the "bottomless abysses," to Snake Field to contemplate the marriage of Snake-Causes with Serpent-Aims.

Here is Pushkin's landscape:

> ...I love the sandstone slope
> Before the hut two rowan trees,
> The gate, the broken fence
> In the sky, grayish clouds...

Here is Vyacheslav Ivanov's landscape:

> You remember: dream masts,
> Like at the docks of Lorrain,
> Rushed up from the fog
> Of river blue
> Toward the ethereal illuminant,
> Where the lunar siren
> Rocked the silver-bosomed,
> Numbing dreams.

As you see, they are in complete antithesis.

Of course, even Vyacheslav Ivanov sometimes speaks of things and phenomena without insisting on the ideas included in them and revealed by the x-rays of his insight, and the above-named poets raised their voices from the transmission of the most secret mysteries,—but neither he nor the others could help feeling like guests, though desired ones, in a sphere foreign to them.

I called the images given by Vyacheslav Ivanov illusory. Really, they are so full, all their component parts so uniformly and intensely bright, that the attention of the reader, unable to grasp the whole, dwells on details, only vaguely suspecting the rest. This gives rise to a feeling of dissatisfaction, but it also forces one to re-

read again and again poems that are already familiar.

Language.... Vyacheslav Ivanov treats it more as a philologist than as a poet. For him, all words are equal, all turns of phrase good; for him there is no secret classification of them into "mine" and "not mine," there are no deep, often inexplicable sympathies and antipathies, He wants to know neither their age nor their country of origin ("in the vernal splash, the cry of the forest soothsayers" and "the whistle of the Harpies in the Lethean swell of the laurel" stand side by side). Like images, they are only the clothing of ideas for him. But his consistently intense thought, his precise knowledge of what he wants to say, make his choice of words so amazingly diverse, that we are justified in speaking of Vyacheslav Ivanov's language as distinct from the language of other poets.

Verse.... Vyacheslav Ivanov handles it perfectly; it seems there is not a single device, however complicated, that he would not know. But for him it is not an aid, not a golden joy, but again only a means. It is not verse that inspires Vyacheslav Ivanov,—on the contrary, he himself inspires his verse. And that is why he loves to write sonnets and ghazals,[2] these difficult and crucial but already formulated verse forms.

I shall speak of the most important thing in Vyacheslav Ivanov's poetry, of that golden staircase along which he leads the fascinated reader, of the content, when the second volume of *Cor Ardens* appears, which should make up a single book with the first.

2

Anthology. Moscow: Musaget, 1911. 2 R.

Of the thirty names found in this almanac of poetry, half are unknown. And at the same time, it contains neither Balmont, nor Sologub, nor Gippius, not to mention the many "young" poets who have already proved themselves. Therefore it is not fair to draw any sort of general conclusions from this book about the fate of Russian poetry. Here the editor did not wish to be a producer, to single out the general from the particular by a skillful distribution of material, or to highlight any one movement by a deliberate choice of names. He was only a censor of literacy and good taste. He fulfilled this humble task well.

The almanac opens with a poem by Vladimir Solovyov, printed for the first time, which is not, however, among his best things.

Vitold Akhramovich[3] contributed four poems: the first inspired by Andrei Bely, the second—by Blok, the third—by Sologub, the fourth—by Kuzmin.

Alexander Blok appears in the full flower of his talent: the way his regal madness fits into sonorous verse is worthy of Byron.

Valerian Borodaevsky recounted some not very interesting themes in not very good poems. He shows a noticeable inclination toward a mechanical production of poems, which was not present in his book.[4]

Andrei Bely's poem "Before an old painting" is beautiful; of the two paths departing from Romanticism—the way of Heine and the way of Goethe—the second, more difficult one served as the inspiration for this poem.

Yury Verkhovsky behaves like a child, but without grace. One line is borrowed from Bryusov.

Eight poems by Maximilian Voloshin.[5] Seven of them are the cycle *Cimmerian Spring*.[6]

Poems by Sergei Gorodetsky dated 1908. Admirers of his poetry will read them with pleasure, while they will dissuade his opponents of nothing.

Four Abyssinian songs by the author of this review, written independently of the real poetry of the Abyssinians.

The ghazals by Vyacheslav Ivanov are a magnificent mosaic of words; his "Spiritual Verses" are perhaps too clearly beautiful for this genre.

P.K. clumsily but openly imitates Kuzmin and Sergei Solovev.

The insipid poem by Samuel Kissin[7] is at least original.

Sergei Klychkov has made progress since the publication of his book.[8] His "Shepherd" is good, and you catch the smell of the sea in his "Fishwife."

In Mikhail Kuzmin's cycle *Autumnal May*, there are fine, classically irreproachable poems that could not have better refuted the author's pessimistic lines:

> All the names are pale, and all titles old,
> But love is always new.
> Can I convey your charm
> When words are so feeble?

Pyotr Potemkin's poems are uneven, as usual, although now there are more successful expressions than unsuccessful ones.

Vladimir Pyast's first poem is magnificent, built on hypnotic, but not tiresome, repetitions. The two others are considerably weaker—as if someone else wrote them.

The Catholic sonnets by Sergei Raevsky[9] are immature, artificial and dull.

One can now find such poems as those of Grigory Rachinsky only in minor weeklies and illustrated supplements to provincial newspapers.

After having raised our hopes, Dmitri Rem contributed poems that were just adequate; one would like to expect something better from him.

Semen Rubanovich is unpleasantly glib, almost impertinent; his lack of taste is not redeemed by novelty of imagery; but he is undoubtedly capable of writing poetry.

Sergei Ryumin[12] arouses no thoughts, fears or hopes; his poems are bad, to put it simply and bluntly.

M.S. is sincere, intelligent, feels deeply, but seems to have too little strength for a poet, although he does know many stylistic devices that make verse alive.

Margarita Sabashnikova's[13] poems, obviously, are born of the author's mysticism, but they are convincing neither as mystical insights nor as poetry.

Boris Sadovskoy is as impersonal as usual, as painstaking as usual. He has ability as well as taste and love for poetry—but not enough of one thing: talent.

The boring knight from *Niva* illustrations[14]—Alexei Sidorov has an equally boring princess; the verse is flaccid; the rhyme *"zhenikh"* with *"ponik"* is incomprehensible.

There are some fine poems among the fourteen by Sergei Solovyov; as always, he was more successful with poems on antique themes than with contemporary ones.

Lyubov Stolitsa's[15] poems are bold, powerful, and finished, but there is a certain lisping voluptuousness in them that creates an unpleasant impression.

Vladislav Khodasevich's poems captivate with their free, sure strokes, their seriousness and their restrained grief; what is more, they are irreproachable in form.

Marina Tsvetaeva's two poems do not add anything to the impression we got from her recently published book.

Ellis writes at length, tediously, with pretentions to refinement and with major blunders.

Apollo, No. 7, 1911.

XX

Northern Flowers for 1911. Collected by "Scorpion" Press, Moscow. 1 R. 50 k.

A year and a half ago the journal *Scales* was discontinued and the "Scorpion" Press, so as not to lose contact with its readers, decided to resume publication of almanacs. The first of them makes a favorable impression. Somov's cover[1] and the familiar names of Bryusov, Balmont, Kuzmin, Gippius and others win the reader over. But upon looking through the collection, and even upon reading it, one feels a certain disappointment. What was good six or seven years ago in *Scales*, reinforced with articles and critiques, seems somehow helplessly unconvincing now. If one excludes the tiny comedy by Mikhail Kuzmin *Liza the Dutchwoman*, with its amusing couplets, two poems by Valery Bryusov, brilliant in conception and execution, and his epic "Underground Dwelling," in which the influences of Dante and Edgar Allan Poe cross in a peculiarly profound way—we are left with nothing which will not irritate us. Zinaida Gippius calls poor assonances "misplaced rhymes," the first instead of the last words in the lines of the poem rhyme—such an obviously artificial vagary can scarcely be called a useful technical innovation and, besides, positively interferes with following the sense of the poems.

How is one to explain to Konstantin Balmont, who has written an essay on Egyptian love poetry, that between the most beautiful words there must be some connection, and that the essence of sugar is bitter to the taste? Here is the first sample of his prose I came across: "The Egyptian dove resembles in its tenderness and delicacy of feeling even more the Hindu paramour, whose name was Radga, and with whose love-fancies and plaints Jayadeva's charming epic is filled..." *Letters of a Russian Traveller*,[3] in comparison with this treacle, is a model of tense style and strict precision of image. In the translation of the Egyptian songs themselves, there is nothing Egyptian—only late Balmont.

The poems by Yurgis Baltrushaitis are well thought out, mature and devastatingly dull.

The poems by D. Navashin,[4] who appears for the first time, apparently, in print, are very poor and, worst of all, promise nothing. His short story "The Pirate" is written in a sugary, insipid style and is almost without any plot.

If it were not for the inappropriate and already tiresome eroticism, Boris Sadovskoy's story "Under Pavel's Shield" would be good.

The foreword is well and vividly written: the motto of the almanac's contributors is stated in it: "faith in the high importance of art as such, which cannot and must not be a means toward anything else, supposedly higher, and a steadfast attempt to serve as best we can precisely this 'higher art'."

Apollo, No. 8, 1911.

XXI

Yurgis Baltrushaitis. *Earthly Stages.* **Moscow: Skorpion. 1 R. 50 k.**
Ilya Ehrenburg. *I Live.* **SPb. 1 R.**
Graal Arelsky. *Blue Azure.* **50 k.**
S. Konstantinov. *Miniatures.* **1 R.**
S. Tartakover. *A Few Poems.* **50 k.**
Alexander Konge and Mikhail Dolinov. *Captive Voices.* **1 R.**
Lev Markovich Vasilevsky. *Poems.* **1 R.**
Alexander E. Kotomkin-Savinsky. *Collected Poems.* **75 k.**
Yury Zubovsky. *Poems.* **Kiev: Lukomore. 85 k.**

Yurgis Baltrushaitis belongs to the older generation of Symbolists, one actually feels in him the stamp of the founders of Skorpion[1] and *Scales:* an elevated, even solemn attitude toward theme and a terseness of verse, although not always in accordance with the significance of the idea.

Baltrushaitis is a Symbolist, but I would rather call him a "metaphorist," if this neologism were not so ugly. In most cases, his poems are only similes, used for the description of an experience and not playing their own non-auxiliary role. Thus, one wants to see the word "like" in front of them, and then a lyrical wave, an epic tale, a sudden breakthrough into real life. But the thick blood of men at the end of the last century prevents the poet from breaking away from the web of metaphors, and his poems, interminably similar to one another, pass by the reader, austere, solemn and unneeded.

Ilya Ehrenburg has made great progress since the publication of his first book.[2] His poems now have neither the childish blasphemy nor the cheap estheticism which, unfortunately, have already managed to poison several beginning poets. He has moved from the ranks of imitators to the ranks of students, and sometimes even sets off on the path of independent creation. In his terze rime,[3] there is a real feeling of paganism, sweet in an earthly sense and slightly miraculous. He skillfully combines lyrical development with historical method, and at the same time almost never raises his voice to a shout. Of course, we have the right to demand a great deal of work from him, especially on language—but the main thing is already accomplished: he knows what poetry is.

Graal Arelsky[4] is one of those poisoned by Ilya Ehrenburg's first book, although his dialogues are more refined, his descriptions more careful. Nevertheless, Igor Severyanin and the contemporary poet-exotics influenced him. There is great naiveté in his predilection for high-ranking persons: infantes, marquis, tsarinas, kings, etc.—all of them lack life. He seems to have no statement of his own which must be spoken at any price, and which alone *makes* a poet, there is only the ardor of youth, an aptitude for versification, taste and knowledge of contemporary poetry. If one thinks of how many writing poetry do not have even these qualities, one cannot help but welcome his appearance.

S. Konstantinov's book made me very happy. Not that there was nothing to criticize. One can criticize it, even ought to—for colorless, unpleasantly polished verse, for thought-slogans already expressed by others, and for the Romantic rubbish, dear to the heart of Graal Arelsky. But it contains a certain genuine, healthy joy in all creation, whimsical, and at the same time stable, images, intoxication with his own and others' strength. Not without reason are three whole poems devoted to the image of Zarathustra. Balmont of the *Burning Buildings* period,[5] and Bryusov, whose influence on the author is very noticeable, make up a fine school. One would like to believe that this is not the last time you will meet with the name of S. Konstantinov is poetry.[6]

It seems that S. Tartokover[7] is also an indubitable poet. He has concentration of thought and great inner experience. He handles the materials of verse skillfully and carefully. But he not only does not feel the Russian language, he does not know it. His syntax is impossible, his vocabulary absurd. "Weakéd, réjected, éxpent, hope succumbs"—such expressions turn up on every page. Judging by these expressions and his last name, S. Tartokover is probably a Jew. He would not be bad if he would just write in Yiddish, like Byalik, Sholom-Ash and others.[8] And then it would be much more interesting to read his poems in translation.

The poems by Alexander Konge[9] and Mikhail Dolinov[10] are preceded by Alexei Kondratev's eloquent foreword: "It is good to be young, to pine for an unearthly, sweet love during the white nights and sing silver sonnets in honor of goddesses and princesses from the kingdom of dreams.... The Muses love young poets.... They know that their young minions are modest, whether they like it or not, and not in any condition to tell a crowd in detail of all the caresses lavished upon them, sometimes they are not even in a condition to sketch the face and the whole outline of the loving Muse who just kissed them...."
It is difficult to add anything to this. To describe both poets is hardly worthwhile. Both of them similarly describe "A White Night," "Forest Roses," "The Evening," "The Moon" (names of poems), etc. The meters are sustained, as are the rhymes. The epithets are accidental and monotonous. A. Konge obviously prefers Blok, Mikhail Dolinov—Bryusov. That is for the readers. As for the authors, one can only advise them to try to awaken the poets in themselves, who are still nowhere in sight.

However strange it may be, the poems of Lev Markovich Vasilevsky[11] have much in common with those of Alexander E. Kotomkin.[12] Even if Vasilevsky writes:

> Twilight, like tentacles, creeps,
> Twilight shrouds the woods,
> in the slow dying vanished
> The echo of minutes slipping away...

And Kotomkin:

> I hear marvelous sounds
> Everything awakes anew.
> The first sorrow of parting
> The first sadness and love.

So what if Vasilevsky mourns over the fate of the Persian woman, who is "at twelve a wife, and at twenty-five an old woman, and drags out her life without the life-giving ray," and Kotomkin joyfully invites the "deceitful world" to listen: "though we are few, brothers, still, all of us are Slavs!...," so what if it becomes clear upon reading their books that Vasilevsky is just as incurable a pessimist as Kotomkin is an optimist. So what if the first writes in a new style, and the second in an old one—they are related by the same lack of striking thoughts, of interesting emotional experiences, of words wrested from the soul, of a reverent attitude toward verse and of everything that we understand by the word poetry.

Yury Zubovsky is young in the good, humane sense. He seethes with images, every sensation new to him he takes as an unearthly revelation, he is intoxicated with himself and those around him. Much of what he says will seem unnecessary and uninteresting, much has already been heard. But there are lines and even stanzas that evoke a joy like spring water, like an unexpectedly discovered flower. As yet he is a vassal—to Blok. But if his inner enthusiasm is not extinguished, he will manage to find his own way.

Apollo, No. 10, 1911.

XXII

Alexander Blok. *Night Hours: Fourth Collection of Poems.* **Moscow: Musaget. 1 R.**
Nikolai Klyuev. *Chime of the Pines.* **Moscow: Znamensky. 60 k.**
Konstantin Dmitrievich Balmont. *Complete Collected Poems.* **Vol. Eight:** *Green Garden.* **Moscow, Skorpion. 1 R. 50 k.**
Paul Verlaine. *Collected Poems.* **Tr. Valery Bryusov. Skorpion.**

Paul Verlaine. *Memoires d'un veuf.* Altsiona. 1 R.
M.G. Veselkova-Kilshtet. *Songs of a Forgotten Estate.* 1 R.
Vadim Shershenevich. *Spring Thaws.* 60 k.
Ivan Genigen. *Poems.* 45 k.

Before Alexander Blok stand two sphinxes that force him "to sing and weep" with their unsolvable riddles: Russia and his own soul. The first is Nekrasovian, the second, Lermontovian. And often, very often, Blok shows them to us, merged into one, organically indivisible. Impossible? But did not Lermontov write "Song of the Merchant Kalashnikov"?[1] From Nekrasov's behests to love the fatherland with sorrow and wrath, he accepted only the first. For example, in the poem "Beyond the Grave," he begins accusingly:

> He was only a fashionable man of letters,
> Only the creator of blasphemous words...

but immediately adds:

> But the dead man is kindred to the people's soul:
> It piously reveres any end...

Or in the poem "Native Land," after the magnificently terrifying lines:

> Beyond the Black Sea, beyond the White Sea
> In black nights and white days.
> Wildly the dumb face stares,
> Tartar eyes cast fire...

The lines that immediately follow bring reconciliation by means of the rhythmic pattern itself, with three adjectives in a row:

> A soft, long, red glow
> Every night above your camp...

This transition from indignation, not to action or appeal, but to harmony (though bought at the price of new pain—the pain is melodious), to, I would say, a Schilleresque beauty, characterizes the Germanic spirit in Blok's works. Before us is not Ilya Muromets, not Alesha Popovich, but a different guest, a renowned hero from across the seas, a sort of Dyuk Stepanovich.[2] And he does not love Russia as a mother, but as a wife, whom one finds when the time comes. In his Lohengringian sorrow, Blok knows absolutely nothing ugly or base to which he could finally say a manly: no! But perhaps he wants to, even seeks it? But an instant later even the theme of the small forgotten station sobs in him like the most sonorous violin:

> The cars went on their usual line,
> Shook and creaked,
> The yellow and red ones were silent,
> In the green ones they wept and sang...

There is a Lermontovian tranquility and melancholy in Blok's purely lyrical poems and confessions, but here also is a characteristic difference: instead of the charming arrogance of a young hussar, he has the noble pensiveness of Michael Cramer. Besides that, one is struck by still another trait in his work, uncharacteristic not only for Lermontov, but for all of Russian poetry in general, namely—morality. Appearing in its initial form as the unwillingness to do evil to another, this morality gives Blok's poetry the impression of a certain peculiar, as well as Schilleresque, humanity.

> For with a candle, in lengthy disquiet
> Her mother does not wait for her at the door,
> For her poor husband behind the thick shutter
> Will not envy her...

he reflects almost at the moment of the embrace and falls in love with the woman for her "youthful contempt" for his desire.

Blok knows, as no one else does, how to unite two themes in one,—not juxtaposing them one to another, but fusing them chemically. In *Italian Poems* there is the majestic and radiant past, and "a certain wind, singing through black velvet of future life," in "Kulikovo Field"—the invasion of the Tatars and the history of an enamoured warrior from among the Russian troops. This device opens limitless horizons for us in the field of poetry.

In general, Blok is one of the wonder-workers of Russian verse. It is difficult to find an analogy to the rhythmic perfection of such poems as "The Pipe Played" or "Today I don't remember."

As a stylist, he does not avoid the usual beautiful words, he knows how to extract from them their original charm.

> Valentina, star, reverie,
> How your nightingales sing...

And his great service to Russian poetry is that he threw off the yoke of exact rhyme and discovered the dependence of rhyme on the initial momentum of the line. His assonances, interspersed in stanzas rhymed throughout, and not just assonances, but simply inexact rhymes, always aim at some sort of especially delicate effect and always achieve it.

This winter brought poetry lovers an unexpected and precious gift. I speak of the book by Nikolai Klyuev,[3] who has been almost unpublished until now. We meet in it a poet who has already reached his full strength, a successor to the tradition of the Pushkin period. His verse is sonorous, clear, full of content. Such a dubious device as that of placing the object before the subject is completely appropriate in his work, and gives his poems a stately firmness and significance. Carelessness of rhyme cannot disturb anyone either, for, as always in great poetry, the center of gravity lies not in the rhymes but in the words within the line. However, such word formations as "imperious-eyed" or "to be many-eyed" makes one recall with pride the same sort of efforts in Yazykov.

The spirit in Klyuev's poetry is rare, exceptional—it is the spirit of one who has found his path.

> Unattainable for death is the bottom,
> And the rivers of life are swift-flowing,—
> But there is a magic wine
> To prolong the enchantment eternally...

he says in one of his first poems, and proves with his whole book that he drank of this wine. He drank, and heavenly springs opened to him, shores of another land, and, emitting blood and flame, the six-winged Archistrategos.[4] Now, lucid, he came to love the world in a new way, snatches of sea foam, the chime of the pines in the rambling forest wilderness and even the gilded sarafans of mature young girls or the Solovetsian belts of fine, burly young men, daredevils and devil-may-cares.

But...

> Only one thing is lacking
> The soul in exile from the vale:
> That the expanses of cornfields, the bosom of waters
> Not resound with a groan of pain...
> . . . .
> And that to steal the crown of the Creator
> Man not endeavor,
> For which, disgraced for eternity,
> I lost the radiant paradise...

Does not this sound like: Glory to God in the highest, and on earth peace, good will toward men?[5] The Slavic feeling of the radiant equality among all people and the Byzantine consciousness of a golden hierarchism in their conception of God. Here, at the sight of the violation of this purely Russian harmony, the poet for the first time experiences grief and wrath. Now he has dreadful dreams:

> As soon as the dusk becomes darker blue,
> And fog shrouds the river—
> Father, with a rope around his neck,
> Will come and sit by the fireside...

Now he knows that cultured society is only "a hollow rumble of a thundering broken wave."

But the Russian spirit is strong, it will always find a way to the light. The leit-motif of the whole book is expressed in the poem "Voice from among the people." To replace the outdated culture which has led us to a dreary atheism and idle spite, people come who can say to themselves: "We are sunrise clouds, the dewy dawns of spring...our chastening father is present in every aspect at every moment...enchanting are our waters and our fire is many-eyed." And what will these radiant warriors do with us, dark, blindly arrogant and blindly cruel? To what torture will they subject us? Here is their answer:

> We, like the streams of underground rivers,
> Shall run to you unseen
> And in a boundless kiss
> Shall fuse fraternal souls.

In the works of Klyuev, the possibility of a truly great epos is taking shape.

Konstantin Balmont is an eternal, disturbing riddle for us. Here he writes a book, then a second, then a third in which there is not a single intelligible image, not a single genuinely poetic page and only in a wild bacchanal rush all these "hundredfold ringings" and "selfimmolatednesses" and other Balmontisms. Critics take up the pen to announce "the end of Balmont"—they love to deliver the *coup de grâce*. And suddenly he publishes a poem, and not just a beautiful one, but an amazing one that rings in your ears for weeks—at the theatre, in a cab, and in the evening before you fall asleep. And then it begins to be seen that perhaps even "selfimmolatedness" and "initially-red Adam"[6] are beautiful, and that only your own insensitivity prevents you from understanding this. But months pass, and despite all the efforts you make, the Balmontisms are not any more familiar and then you again begin to get used to the strange idea that even a very great poet can write very bad poetry. But still it is dreadful...

However, these fears need not concern the reader, and, speaking of Balmont, the critic always runs the risk of being taken in. In *Green Garden* there is this amazingly beautiful poem—"Starfaced":

> His face was like the Sun—at that hour when the Sun
> > is at its zenith,
> His eyes were like stars—before they fall from the heavens...

and farther on:

> "I am the first," quoth he, "and the last"—and booming
> > thunder answered.
> "The hour of reaping," said the Starry-eyed—"Prepare the
> > scythes. Amen."
> We in a faithful crowd arose, in the sky the fractures glowed red,
> And seven golden heptastera led us to the border of
> > the wilderness.

Green Garden (Kissed Words) was inspired in Balmont by the songs and legends of the Khlysty.[7] Many poems are simply imitations. Of course, their genuine religious flavor was lost in Balmont, who could never distinguish heavenliness from airiness. But there are stanzas in which their inherent naïveté is beautifully reproduced, for example in the poem about the Tree of Paradise:

> But the only evil in it,
> Is that there is a prohibition,
> O fatal tree,
> You sow rebellion...

or slyness:

> We are, not according to the law,
> We are by grace.
> Having illumined the icon,
> We lie down on the bed.

or, finally, the wildly energetic expressions:

> I give him my curse,
> I give him my threefold curse,
> My fourfold curse I give.

A strange fate befell Verlaine. Somehow, the previous generation, just after a long period of inattention, pronounced him their *maître*, his name was a motto, they were absorbed in reading his poems. Even now the graying Symbolists like René Ghil, having magnanimously forgotten past quarrels, devote whole studies to him. But the young generation of Frenchmen, in the persons of their most brilliant representatives, stubbornly refuse to think about him. And so with us. Of the Modernists only Bryusov, Annensky and Sologub have translated him. Youth is silent. There can be many explanations for this fact. For example: Symbolism in its beginnings had much in common with Romanticism, broadened, deepened, ennobled. And Verlaine is a direct successor of Villon,[8] so dear to the Romantics. He was sincere, amorous, freely elegant, devout and depraved,—really, a charming figure for those times when people had a supply of gay thoughtless energy, not dissipated by their drowsy fathers, the Parnassians or the tongue-tied poets of our Eighties. Youth does not have such a rich legacy, but the habit of gaiety has remained, and for that reason, it more strictly chooses its favorites, demanding from them sweeping plans and their fitting execution, conscientious and productive efforts and not childish enthusiasm, but the sacred fire of Prometheus. Verlaine, obviously, did not have this. His poetry is a lyrical *intermezzo*, precious as a human document and a description of the era, but only that.

Valery Bryusov's book gives a full idea of Verlaine as a poet. A perfect knowledge of all his poetry allowed the translator to use Verlaine's own vocabulary in those passages where exactness of translation is unthinkable. Many stanzas, even poems , vie with the original in charm.

The translations from *Romances sans paroles*[9] turned out especially well. The article included in the book is of exhaustive nature.

Memoires d'un veuf,[10] published by "Altsiona" Press, serves as a fine supplement to Bryusov's book, for a more full acquaintance with Verlaine. Verlaine is no less fascinating as a prose writer than as a poet. A series of extremely witty paradoxes, unexpected images and moments of purely French aristocratic delicacy scattered through the whole book makes reading it captivating.

The poems of Mrs. Veselkova-Kilshtet have one unquestionable virtue: their theme. It is an elegant idea to devote a whole book to the poetry of forgotten estates, so touchingly forlorn, scattered through great and terrible Russia. The author has both knowledge of her theme and love for it. There are entirely successful poems and excellent individual stanzas.

For example, a girl's languor in the poem "Patience":

> For Grandfather I lay out the cards,
> And he watches. King and ace...
> Oh, heart, your king is in the garden,
> And in vain I yearn for him.

But one is unpleasantly struck in this book by the lack of purely literary aims of, to some degree, interesting artistic devices. And the stamp of dilettantism, even if of a clever and talented sort, lies indelibly upon it.

Vadim Shershenevich[11] is entirely under the influence of Balmont's poetry. But, perhaps this is the most natural path for a young poet. There is neither slackness nor bad taste in his poems, but neither is there strength or novelty. He has only announced that he exists by this book, and one can accept that fact without a scornful grimace. But he must still prove that he lives as a poet.

How often people take an abundance of ideas, a wealth and diversity of impressions as poetic talent. It is precisely in the absence of it that these very qualities prevent a person from becoming even a decent versifier. He gets lost in periods, breaks the most immutable laws of poetry, lapses into bad taste and bad grammar and all—to more precisely express the thought or sensation dear to him. Such is Ivan Genigin. Only great refinement would show him that he is not a poet. But that is the very thing he is lacking.

Apollo, No. 1, 1912.

XXIII

Valery Bryusov. *Mirror of Shadows: Poems.* Moscow: Skorpion, 1912. 2 R.
Mikhail Zenkevich. *Wild Purple: Poems.* Tsekh Poetov, 1912. 90 k.
Elizaveta Kuzmina-Karavaeva. *Scythian Shards: Poems.* Tsekh Poetov, 1912. 90 k.
Georgy Ivanov. *Embarkation for the Island of Cythera:*[1] *Poesies.* Ego, 1912. 50 k.

Probably more has been written about Valery Bryusov than about any other contemporary poet, and probably there is no one else with whom representatives of the most diverse movements are angry. One cannot help but admit that they all have a right to be, for Bryusov enticed each of them in turn with the hope of calling him their own; and having enticed them, slipped away. But how terrible: we do not perceive his work as a conglomeration of poems dissimilar to each other, but, on the contrary, he seems unified, harmonious, indivisible. It is not eclecticism: stern poverty rather than frivolous diversity expresses the distinctive trait of Bryusov's themes. Here we have something different. It is no wonder that the words "Bryusovian school" sound just as natural and clear as Parnassian school" or "Romantic school." Indeed, a conqueror but not an adventurer, careful but not decisive, as calculating as a brilliant strategist, Valery Bryusov assimilated the characteristic traits of all literary schools that existed before him, perhaps through "euphuism" inclusive. But he added a certain something to them that made them blaze with a new fire and forget previous quarrels. Perhaps this something is the basis of a new school coming to replace Symbolism; after all, Andrei Bely did say that Bryusov transmits his precepts over the heads of his contemporaries. *Mirror of Shadows*, more vividly than other books, reflects this statement, which is new, consequently belonging to tomorrow.

> For all the lyre prophesied to us,
> All by which the eye was moved in colors,
> For the proud visages of Shakespeare,
> For Raphael's madonnas—
> We must be on the watch of peace,
> Sacred for all times.

In these simple and extremely noble lines, Bryusov emphasizes his neither bestial nor divine, but simply human, nature, a love of culture in its most vivid and characteristic manifestations. Apparently at first the poet, considered a Symbolist, invoked Raphael instead of Botticelli, Shakespeare instead of Marlowe. That shows a synthetic understanding of the nineteenth century, so desecrated and so heroic. And now the words of Daedalus, once irritating, always intriguing, sound for us anew (the poem "Daedalus and Icarus") in *Garland*:

> My son, my son, fly midway
> Between the first heaven and the earth.

Not one of the achievements of the human spirit is lost with such an attitude toward poetry. In this world, simple and clear, when you see it from an automobile, there are miracles as indisputable and accessible to all, as "rain-washed groves," or "vales, where the forest is dark." Here is *Le paradis artificiel.*

> Languor of a secret hangover
> Caresses my drowsiness,
> Neither rapture, nor mirth,
> Nor the sweetness of caresses are sharp.

But these miracles (perhaps like all miracles) lead the tempted to the country of "the unknown Gobi, where despair is the name of the capital."

Such realization of each image and absolute honesty with oneself, is this not a dream for us, so recently freed from the fetters of Symbolism? And this dream is no longer a dream for Bryusov.

From Bryusov's wise Daedalus, soaring "between the first heaven and the earth," we move to Mikhail Zenkevich,[2] a free hunter, who does not want to know anything, except the earth. His appeal to the air we can apply to the whole of the other world:

> ...O, air, free element,
> Viscous, earthly armor!
> Do not submit, like the others—
> Water, earth and fire.
>
> In their abysses we imagine emptiness,
> And with hooting, like an idol,
> Bound to a horse's tail
> That god, who betrayed the secret...

Where the demands of composition force him to turn to eternity and God, he feels out of his element, and always suspects them of some sort of injustice. Thus, in the poem "Butcher Stalls," having described the slaughterhouse with lush, daring realism, he exclaims:

> And it seems that in the golden ether
> The Scales weigh us just like the meat,
> And the pans are just as rusty, the weights as heavy,
> And the dogs just as greedily lick up crumbs.

He is completely content with the earth, but we do not have the heart to reproach him for this self-restriction, because the earth is really good to him and reveals itself before him fully and intimately. When he addresses water, stones and metals in the second person, we feel that he bought this right with great knowledge, born of great love. And the heroes of his poems—Commodus, Ahura-Mazdah or Alexander of Macedon[3]—they are no longer men, but "granite gods, carved with copper in the mountains."

And his warning to man resounds like the reminder of a great truth we have forgotten:

> Forge the elements in incandescent heat,
> But with your soul, proud Tsar, be reconciled
> And from the last slimy creature
> Learn dark insight!

Elizaveta Kuzmina-Karavaeva is one of those poets with an *idée fixe*. Her task is to create a Scythian epos, but there is still too much youthful lyricism in her soul, too little of the defined and, therefore daring, talent's ability to judge by sight and resolution. Play of metaphors, sometimes not just verbal ones, firm dogmatism of a vaguely mystical character, and naively hieratical poses—all this is little help in creating an epos. Only shards of it remain, but, to the honor of the poet, genuine Scythian shards.

> I look, I look from the lonely tower.
> Ah, to sleep, to sleep eternally!
> The black spots of Russian fields,
> The hoisted sails of a Turkish vessel.

With this definition of Russia as something far away, unnecessary, reflection takes hold of us, is it really our homeland, and didn't we know sometime long ago another homeland, some free, ancient, grassy Scythia. For Kuzmina-Karavaeva it is the promised land, paradise, and perhaps for us as well. So, in people's lives many mystical revelations are explained simply by a sudden recollection of scenes which made a strong impression on us in early childhood. The same thing probably happens in the life of a race.

A general illusoriness in combination with a hypnotic preciseness of some one detail is the distinctive characteristic of Kuzmina-Karavaeva's poetry.

> Off in the distance—a tree in smoke
> And the illusoriness of the seas.
> Now I know that I shall understand
> The mute speech of beasts.

This is purely the psychology of a dream.
I think that these shards have a fair chance of merging into a

whole vessel, preserving the precious chrism of poetry, but this will scarcely happen quite as quickly as the author thinks, because the external plot of the book, the story of the love of a slave-princess for her master, seems, to modern taste, unconvincing and accidental against the truly ancient and strange outlines of the landscape.

The first thing that attracts attention in Georgy Ivanov's book is the verse. Rarely is it so refined in beginning poets, now impetuous and quick, more often only slow, always in accordance with the theme. For this reason, reading each poem gives an almost physical feeling of satisfaction. Reading carefully, we find other great merits: indisputable taste even in the most daring endeavors, unexpectedness of theme and a certain graceful "silliness" in the same measure tha Pushkin demanded it. Then, there is the development of images in the poem Early Spring": "in the verdure mourns a marble cupid," but he does not mourn simply, as he mourned in the dozens of poems by other poets, but "mourns, that his flesh is stone." In another poem: the sun "with the flat of his sword—magnificent radiance—struck the earth." This indicates great concentration of artistic observation and compels one to believe in the future of the poet. In regard to theme, Georgy Ivanov is wholly under the influence of Mikhail Kuzmin. The same unusual transitions from the "beautiful clarity" and mocking delicacy of the eighteenth century to rapturously ringing poem-prayers. But of course the imitation is inferior to the original in complexity, strength and depth.

Apollo, Nos. 3-4, 1912.

XXIV

Marina Tsvetaeva. *Magic Lantern: Second Book of Poems.* Moscow: Ole-lukoie, 1912. I R. 50 k.
Pavel Radimov. *Field Psalms: Poems.* Kazan, 1912. 1 R. 25 k.
Vsevolod Kurdyumov. *Azra: Poems.* SPb. 60 k.
Anatoly Burnakin. *Parting: Song-book.* Moscow, 1912. 50 k.
Sasha Cherny. *Satires and Lyric.* Book Two. SPb.: Shipovnik.
Pyotr Potemkin. *Geranium.* SPb.: M.G. Kornfeld, 1912.

The path of genius runs free and clear from theme to theme, from device to device, but always to the same eternal, great Self.... Through rigorous toil, constant effort, talent achieves diversity, without which there can be no great work. And it is always sad to see a real poet search carefully and painstakingly, wishing to move away from what he has already found, and renounce the redeeming dizziness of a conqueror.

Marina Tsvetaeva's first book, *Evening Album*,[1] compelled one to believe in her, and perhaps most of all in her unfeigned childlike qualities, so sweetly, naively unaware of their distinctions from maturity. *Magic Lantern*, though, is an imitation, and what is more, published by a stylized publishing-house "for children," in whose catalogue a total of three books are marked. The same themes, the same images, only paler and drier, as if these were not experiences and not memories of things experienced, but merely memories of memories. The same with regard to form. The verse no longer flows gaily and carelessly as before; it drifts and breaks off, and the poet tries to replace inspiration with an ability, alas, still too inadequate. There are no more long poems—as if she were short of breath. The short ones are often built on repetition or paraphrase of the same line.

They say that a young poet's second book is usually the least successful. We will count on that....

Pavel Radimov, as far as I know, is appearing in print for the first time.[2] It is wonderful to see that in his book there are all the qualities necessary for a good poet, although they are still not bound together, and although there is much backsliding and awkwardness. This is material, but valuable material on which one can and should work.

The author approaches his theme boldly and, good or bad, tries to make use of it to the end. It seems that the French poets influenced him. At least in his primitive poems one hears from time to time now Rosny,[3] now Leconte de Lisle,[4] and, reading the beautiful poem about the sexton and his dog, you remember Francis Jammes[5] without disappointment.

Vsevolod Kurdyumov's poems[6] are constructed as if they were to be declaimed from a provincial stage. Gloomy romanticism, tearful sensitivity and a light touch of civic spirit—they have everything.... The spirited endings must provoke rapture in the

110

gallery. But Russian literature is not a provincial state. Vsevolod Kurdyumov must discard a great deal, a very great deal, and gain even more if he wants to enter literature.

If the name Anatoly Burnakin[7] meant nothing to me, if I believed in the authenticity of his song-book, how I would fear for the contemporary creative work of the people, how un-Russianly sweet and weak it would seem to me. But fortunately, I know that Burnakin, a former Modernist, is now a new-style critic, and I can have no doubts of the intellectual origins of the song-book. Still, it is unfortunate that a Russian critic fails to smell the aroma of folk poetry to such an extent that he thinks to imitate it with any means he possesses.

Another intellectual, Sasha Cherny,[8] is more likeable in that he puts on no mask, and writes as he thinks and feels; and he is not to blame that it comes out pathetic and ridiculous. For future ages, his book will be a valuable aid in the study of the dilettante period in Russian life. For contemporaries it is a collection of all that is most hateful to long-suffering but hardy Russian culture.

Pyotr Potemkin's poems are to poetry what caricature is to drawing. There are special laws for them, charming and unexpected. It seems the poet has finally found himself. With amazing ease and speed, but the speed of a pencil and not a camera, he sketches the grotesques of our city, always surprising, always true to life. A slight melancholy smile, which is felt in every poem, only increases their artistic value. The so-called "serious" poems, for example "Persian Geranium," several from "Masquerade" and others, are less interesting.

Apollo, No. 5, 1912.

XXV

Vyacheslav Ivanov. *Cor Ardens.* **Part Two. Skorpion. —Nikolai Klyuev.** *Fraternal Songs.* **Book Two. —Vladimir Narbut.** *Halleluiah: Poems.* **Tsekh Poetov. —Count Pyotr Bobrinsky.** *Poems.* **SPb. —Oscar Wilde.** *The Sphinx.* **Tr. Alexander Deich. Maski.**

For a long time Vyacheslav Ivanov, as a poet, has been a riddle for me. What sort of poems are these, that equally unfoundedly, some wisely praise, others abuse? Whence this artfulness and floridity, and at the same time authenticity of language, affected even according to the rules of Latin syntax? How is one to explain this monotonous intensity, which gives a purely intellectual delight and which completely excludes the "unexpected joy" of the accidentally discovered image, of momentary inspiration? Why do we constantly and everywhere find instead of the poet's lyrical surprise at his experiences—"is it really so?"—an epic (perhaps even didactic), omniscient—"so it had to be"?

And only while reading the second part of *Cor Ardens*, the section entitled *Rosarium*,[1] did I understand what the problem is....

The most sensitive foreigners are convinced that Russians are a completely unique, strange people. The mystery of the Slavic soul—*l'âme slave*—is a generality in the West. But they satisfy thmselves with a description of its contradictions. We Russians should go further, searching for the sources of these contradictions. Undoubtedly, we are not just a transition from the psychology of the East to the psychology of the West, or vice versa, we are indeed a whole and complete organism, the proof of which is in Pushkin; but among us, normally, there are reversions to the purity of one of these types. Thus Bryusov is always and completely a European in each line of his poetry, in each of his journal notices. I would like to show that Vyacheslav Ivanov is from the East. Tradition does not say whether the *Tsar-magus* Gaspar composed songs. But if he did it seems to me that they would have been similar to Vyacheslav Ivanov's poems. When he rode by night on his decorated camel, seeing the same sands and the same stars, when even the guiding star leading to Bethlehem became ordinary and everyday, he sang songs, ancient, slow, their melodies reminiscent of the five and six-foot iambs, the favorite meter of Vyacheslav Ivanov.... Being very wise, for him the joy of learning was already ended, for him there was neither preference nor hate, and the things, ideas and names (ah, they are only *Maya*,[2] a deceptive illusion) in these songs rose and fell like shadows. And just as he, for the sake of sonorous names or secondary associations invoked heroes forgotten by us, without a moment's hesitation over them, so Vyacheslav Ivanov speaks now about Francis of Assisi, now about Perseus[3] in one and the same poem, because both are for him only *Maya* and at best, symbols. The style is the man—but who does not know Vyacheslav Ivanov's style with its solemn archaisms, sharp *enjambements*, accentuated alliteration and an arrangement of words which thoroughly eclipses the general meaning of the sentence. A ponderous splendor, stupefying, barbaric, as if the poet were not a willful child but the Persian emperor Basileus[4] in the imagination of the ancient Greeks.

That this stylization of Eastern poets is not a vulgar *partis pris* is shown by the poet's unconscious gravitation, according to the law of repulsion, toward typically Western images and forms. There are sonnets in the book, *canzoni, ballades, rondeaux, rondelles,* you could not list them all; images of the Renaissance and ancient Greece are most common; Italy dominates the poet's dreams, even the epigraphs are almost all Italian. But in all these poems, one senses a distinguished foreigner, for whom the laws of the country are not obligatory, who admires, but does not love, is interested but does not know, and haughtily refuses to change. Only in the poems devoted to the East, and perhaps in the native Russian ones, also strongly tinted with Eastern coloring and reminiscent in their gaudy pattern of Persian rugs, only in them do you find strength and simplicity, proving that the poet is at home, in his native land.

How should one regard Vyacheslav Ivanov? Of course a great, distinctive individuality is most valuable of all. But for others to follow him who do not possess his gifts would be to enter upon a risky, perhaps even fatal venture. He is dear to us, as an exponent of one of the extremes found in the Slavic soul. But, protecting the integrity of Russian ideas, we must, while loving this extreme, persistently say "no" to it, and remember that it is not by accident that the heart of Russia is simple Moscow, and not splendid Samarkand.

Even now, neither criticism nor the public knows how to regard Nikolai Klyuev. What is he—an exotic bird, a strange grotesque, only a peasant by some amazing chance writing irreproachable poems, or the herald of a new power, of folk culture?

With the publication of his first book *Chime of the Pines,*[5] I said the latter; *Fraternal Songs* strengthens me in my opinion. The author says of them in the preface: "For the most part, they were composed before my first book, or at the same time. They were not included in the first book because they had not been written down by me, but transmitted orally or in written form, without my knowledge..." Models of folk art take shape in exactly this way, somewhere in the forest, on the road, where there is neither the possibility nor the desire to write them down, polish them, where it is impossible to attach a clumsy ending to a successful stanza, to forgo not only grammar, but meter. Klyuev's inspiration is always the same, deeply religious.

> The echo of the bells, now resonantly clear,
> Now staccato golden, bewitches and intoxicates.
> Who is this, to one side, majestically meek,
> In the clothes of a foreigner, standing outcast?

For Klyuev, Christ is a leitmotif not only of poetry, but of life. This is not sectarianism, by no means, this is the natural striving of a lofty soul toward the heavenly Bridegroom.... Monasticism, asceticism are antithetical to it, it will not allow Mary to offend gentle Martha:

> Unmourned is the past,
> For love unforgiven,
> Guard the earthly, child,
> If heaven is not given.

But it does have a proud consciousness, which places it above the everyday.

> We are the heralds of Christ,
> The first-born of Adam.

The introductory article by Valentin Sventsitsky goes astray precisely in its sectarian narrowness and unfoundedness. Revealing every allusion, philosophically basing every metaphor, it cheapens Nikolai Klyuev's work, reducing him to a restatement of the doctirnes of the Golgothian Church.[7]

The first generation of Russian Modernists incidentally, were also fascinated with estheticism. Their poems teemed with beautiful, often vapid words and names. They really have, as Balmont said, "sounds, colors and flowers, aromas and dreams, all combined in an harmonious choir, all woven into one pattern." A reaction arose in the second generation (with Bely and Blok), but such an indecisive one that it soon died out. The third generation ended this trend. Mikhail Zenkevich and even more, Vladimir Narbut came to hate not only vapid, beautiful words, but all beautiful words; not only hackneyed refinement, but any sort at all: their attention was attracted by everything that was really outcast, the slime, dirt and soot of the world. But where Zenkevich softens the shameless reality of his images with the mist of remote times or remote lands, Vladimir Narbut is consistent to the end, although perhaps not without mischief. Here, for example, is the beginning of his poem "Evil Creature."

> A sharp pain in the small of the back,
> Pokes with an awl in the right side:
> Of a stumpy gnome dreams
> A spry wench—forehead sweaty.
> He presses, runs closer,
> Roars, a second and he'll grab:
> The damp foot-clothes stink of
> stables, rusty swamps etc.

Hallucinating realism!

It would seem like a simple *Kunstkammer*,[8] this whole selection of strong, earthy, solid vocabulary, these little Ukrainian words, unexpected, sometimes clumsy rhymes, rather coarse stories—if it were not for the poem "The Fortune-Teller." In it is an explanation of the poet's dream, bewitched and captivated by the subjects surrounding it.

> Tearful old woman by the window
> Snuffles at me, spreading my hand:
> "You've lived your days, and will live them—alone.
> But some sort of separation awaits you..."
> All sooty, the incalculable load
> Of the years she carries on her stooped back—
> She reminded me of campestrian Rus
> (Feather-grass and camps), when she glanced,
> And the earthy, evil witchcraft
> Was so transparent, that I humbly
> Without tears, without malice accepted it,
> Like a field in autumn, the ripened grain.

115

And in every poem we feel diverse manifestations of the same earthy, evil witchcraft, elemental and bewitching with the new and genuine fascination of ugliness.[9]

Those who love to grumble insist that in our time it has become very easy to write poetry. They are partly right—we really are experiencing a poetic Renaissance. Special attention is paid to poetry, to be interested in it is considered elegant, and it is not suprising that more and more of it appears.... But to write good poetry now is just as difficult as always. Take for example Count Pyotr Bobrinsky.[10] His poems are metrically correct, neat in rhyme, rather figurative, but they have neither strength nor moderation nor a proper alternation between light and shadow, everything that we are accustomed to demand of poems to consider them poetry. In uncultured circles, it is customary to consider such sheer prettiness to be estheticism. But then that is the same as calling a man who eats sugar by the spoonful an epicure.

This is a dangerous sign, and one can sooner forgive amusing slips of the pen like "the basalt couch of roses," feelings carried "beneath the heart," "jagged armor,"[11] or the couplet "in a rush—gods, we proudly ordered our Don stallions to be saddled." All this indicates only the extreme youth of the author and keeps us from passing a final verdict.

The translation by Alexander Deich of Wilde's famous poem *The Sphinx*[12] undoubtedly deserves to be mentioned. It is the first to be done in the author's meter and to be fairly close to the English.

However, Wilde's *Sphinx* is not only an interestingly conceived work, but a splendidly executed one as well, and as one of the strongest means of influencing the reader, one which best conveys lyric emotion, the poet employs the carry-over of a sentence from one stanza to another. There are several of them in the poem, and each time these carry-overs signify a change of theme. The translator, in his efforts to be literal, did not notice this and gave only a very conscientious paraphrase. One ought to be thankful for that much.

Apollo, No. 6, 1912.

XXVI

Alexander Blok. *Collected Poems in Three Volumes.* **Book 1:**
Poems of the Beautiful Lady. **Book II:** *Unexpected Joy.*
Book III: *Snowy Night.* **Moscow: Musaget.**
Mikhail Kuzmin. *Autumn Lakes.* **Second book of Poems. Moscow:**
Scorpion.

Usually, a poet gives people his creative works. Blok gives
people himself.

By this I mean to say that in his poems he not only doesn't
resolve some sort of general problems, be they literary (as in Pushkin), philosophical (as in Tyuchev), or social (as in Hugo), but that
he doesn't even indicate them, and that he simply describes his
own life, which fortunately for him is so marvelously rich with
internal struggle, catastrophes and enlightenment.

"I did not listen to tales, I am a simple man," says Pierrot[1] in
"Harlequin," and one would like to see these words as an epigraph
to all three books of Blok's poems. At the same time he has a
purely Pushkinian ability to give a feeling for the eternal in the
momentary, to show the shadow of the genius watching over his
fate behind ever accidental image. I said that this is a Pushkinian
ability and will not take back these words. Is not even the *Gavril-
iad*[2] imbued with a perhaps strange, but still religious sensation
more than many plump volumes of various Words and Reflection? Are not Pushkin's album verses a sacred hymn of the mysteries of the new Eros?

There has been much conjecture about the Blokovian Beautiful Lady—people have wished to see in her now Woman, clothed in
the Sun, now the Eternal Feminine, now a symbol of Russia. But
if one were to believe that this is simply the girl with whom the
poet was in love for the first time, it seems to me that not one
poem in the book would refute this opinion, and the image itself,
grown more familiar, will become even more miraculous and will
gain infinitely from this in the artistic sense. We understand that in
this book, as in Dante's *La Vita Nuova,* de Ronsard's *Sonnets,*
Goethe's *Werther* and Baudelaire's *Les Fleurs du Mal,*[3] a new visage of love is revealed to us; a love which wants blindness, feeds on
forebodings, believes omens and sees unity in everything because it
sees only itself; a love which once again proves that man is not just
an ape in perfected form. And we shall be on the side of the poet

117

when he, with the mouth of that same Pierrot, screams to the mystics gathered round him: "You won't fool me, this is Columbine, this is my bride!" In the second book, Blok seems to have looked about at the world of objects surrounding him for the first time, and having looked about, become indescribably joyful. Hence the title. But this was the beginning of tragedy. Credulously enraptured with the world, forgetting the difference between it and himself, a live soul, the poet, somehow at once and in a strange way accepted and loved everything easily—the swamp priest, occupied with God knows what in the swamp, but hardly only with treating frogs' feet, the dwarf holding back the pendulum with his hand and with it killing a child, and imps, pleading not to be taken to the Holy Places, and in the depths of this questionable kingdom, as queen, in silks and rings, the Mysterious Ladies, Hysteria and her servant Alcohol.

The Mysterious Lady is the leitmotif of the whole book. This is a false promise of materialization that will afford perfect happiness and the impossible, but it is not pure and mute like the stars, whose sense and truth lie in the fact that they are unattainable,— rather it is seductive and enticing, disquieting as the moon. This is the siren of the city, demanding that those in love with her renounce their soul.

But the poet with the heart of a child, Blok, did not want to embark upon such conciliatory adventures. He preferred death. And half of *Snowy Night*, that which earlier made up *Earth in Snow*,[4] contains a constant and persistent thought of death, not of the next world but only of the moment of passing into it. *The Masque of Snow* is that same Mysterious Lady, simply despairing of her victory and, in invitation, desiring destruction for the lover slipping away from her. And in the poems of this period, one hears not only hysterical ecstasy or hysterical torment, one already feels in them the solemn approach of the Spirit of Music, conquering the demons. Music is what unites the earthly world with the incorporeal world. It is the soul of objects and the body of thought. In the violins and bells of *Night Hours* (the second half of *Snowy Night*), there is no longer hysteria—the poet has successfully passed through that period. All the lines are firm and precise, and at the same time not one image is delineated to the point of retreat into itself, all are alive in the full sense of that word, all are palpitating, they toss and drift into the "native land of worldly violins." Words are like notes, phrases are like chords. And the world, ennobled with music, became humanly beautiful and pure—all of it, from the grave of Dante to the faded curtains above sick geraniums. Into what forms Blok's poetry will flow next, I think no one, least of all Blok himself, can say.

The poetry of Mikhail Kuzmin is for the most part "salon" poetry—not that it is not genuine or beautiful poetry, on the contrary, "salon-ness" is given to it as some extra quality making it unlike others. It has responded to everything that for some years past has excited the drawing rooms of Petersburg. The eighteenth century from Somov's point of view, the Thirties, Russian schismatism, and everything that has occupied literary circles: ghazals, French *ballades*, acrostics and occasional verse. And one feels that all this is first-hand, that the author was not following the vogue, but took part in its creation himself.

Like *Nets*, Mikhail Kuzmin's first book,[5] *Autumn Lakes* is almost exclusively devoted to love. But instead of the former tender wit and intimacy so characteristic of love, we find impassioned eloquence and the somewhat solemn seriousness of sensual attraction. The bonfire has flared up and, from a welcoming flicker, it has become majestic. Even if all the familiar places are mentioned—Boisson's photographic studio, Moscow's "Metropol"[6]— it is clear to the reader that only one ancient image dominates the dreams of the poet, the mythological *Amour*, the marvelously animated "naked lad in a field of rye" shooting golden arrows. The poet divines him, and only him, both in a fashionable dinner jacket and beneath the regulation cocked hat. This even explains the repetition, rather strange in contemporary poetry, of the words "bow," "arrows," "pierce," "prick," that under other conditions would seem like intolerable rhetoric.

This very same *Amour* with a traditional quiver flies down to the poet at noon from a golden cloud and sits with him in the noisy hall of a restaurant. Both here and there—the same "familiar visage." It is madness, yes, but it has another name too—poetry.

Somewhat detached but in profound inner accordance with the whole stands the section of Eastern ghazals—"Spring Garland" and "Spiritual Verses," together with "Day of the Most Holy Virgin." In the first, covered by the shadow of Hafiz,[6] the impassioned eloquence of sensuality of which I spoke earlier was successfully harmonized with the bright colors of Eastern nature, bazaars and festivals. Mikhail Kuzmin passed by the heroic poetry of

the Bedouins and settled upon the poetry of their urban followers
and successors, which is well-suited to refined rhythms, affected
difficulty of locution and magnificence of vocabulary. In his Russian poems, the second face of sensuality—its solemn seriousness—
became religious lucidity, simple and wise beyond any stylization.
It is as though the poet himself prayed in Volga-side cloisters and
lit lamps before ikons of antique design. He, who feels in everything the reflection of Another, be it God or Love, he has the right
to speak these triumphal lines:

> I do not believe the sun that moves toward nightfall.
> I do not believe the summer that moves toward decline,
> I do not believe the cloud that darkens the vale,
> Nor a dream do I believe—death in the form of a monkey.
> I do not believe the deceitful ebb of the sea,
> The flower I do not believe, that insists: "she loves me not!"

Mikhail Kuzmin holds one of the first places among contemporary Russian poets. Only a few are blessed with such an amazing
harmony of the whole, combined with free diversity of details. As
a spokesman, however, for the views and feelings of a whole circle
of people united by a common culture and by rights ascended to
the crest of life, he is a poet of this earth, and finally, his fully developed technique never overshadows the image, but only inspires
it.

XXVII

Sergei Gorodetsky. *Willow: Fifth Book of Poems.* SPb.: Shipovnik, 1913. 2 R.
Vladimir Bestuzhev. *Return.* SPb.: Tsekh Poetov, 1913. 1 R. 20 k.

Sergei Gorodetsky is a great joy to all of us. He appeared in
literature only seven years ago and has already managed to do so
much that one is dazzled. A series of poetry books, several books
of short stories, poems and tales for children, articles on questions
of literature, painting, theory of art, translations, prefaces—in a
word, in all spheres where the opportunity presents itself of think-

ing and speaking out, Sergei Gorodetsky. This lack of restraint in creative power, absence of vacillation in executing what has been conceived, and this uniformity of style in the most different endeavors reveals an impetuous and strong nature, completely fitting for the heroic twentieth century.

Sergei Gorodetsky began as a Symbolist, then declared himself an advocate of mythopoeism, and now he is an "Acmeist." In *Willow* there are poems marked with the stamp of each of these three periods. Symbolist poems in which the image, by comparison with rhythm, plays a purely secondary role, are weaker than the others. Having touched the heart of Slavdom, Sergei Gorodetsky feels tht the measure of verse is not the boot, but the image, as in Russian songs and *byliny*, [1] and however strong the experience or deep the thought, they cannot become the material of poetic creation until they are clothed in the live and tangible flesh of the image, active and valuable in itself. Hence the insipidity and slackness of his Symbolist endeavors, for Symbolism is now simply a literary school, one that has finished its cycle of development, and not a voice on the road to Damascus as it was for the first Symbolists....

The mythopoeic period of Sergei Gorodetsky is very significant first of all because the poet fell into error, thinking that mythopoeism is the natural outcome of Symbolism, while it is a decisive departure from it. Myth is the self-contained image, having its own name, developing in internal accordance with itself— and what could be more odious for the Symbolists who see in the image only an allusion to "the great facelessness," to chaos, Nirvana or the void? Therefore we will not apply the Symbolist method to mythopoeism. Sergei Gorodetsky's failure showed us that. His "Verines" (interestingly conceived and deeply felt, thanks to the impressionism of the account and the absence of perspective) is only a story of events and not the events themselves, and we can only *trust* that everything was just as the poet relates, but not *believe* in it.

Dreaming of myth, Sergei Gorodetsky understood that a different school was indispensable for him, one more rigorous and fruitful, and he turned to *Acmeism.* Acmeism (from the word *acme*—the full development of all spiritual and physical powers) in essence is mythopoeism. Because what, if not myths, will the poet create who has repudiated both the exaggeration peculiar to youth and uninspired, senile moderation, who strains all the powers of his spirit uniformly, who accepts the word in all its dimensions, musical, pictorial and ideological—who demands that every creation be a microcosm. Criticism has more than once noted a predominance of subject over predicate among the Symbolists. Acmeism found this predicate in the development of the image-idea, logically musical, uninterrupted throughout the whole poem.

"Wanderers," "The Beggar," "Wolf" represent the masculine element of Acmeism in Sergei Gorodetsky's poems, the cycle *Tormenting Life*—the feminine. It seems to me that the latter is more familiar to the poet. Because, despite the splendid fervor and terseness of expression in poems of the first category, there is in them a certain softness and delicate reverie that best of all defines the author himself.

> ...As if sounds are all amorous
> ...And all words tender.

Vladimir Bestuzhev[2] began his poetic activities with the early Russian Symbolists and only this year was his first book published. In this, and in much else he resembles Yury Baltrushaitis. However, Baltrushaitis, after all, took part in the life of his circle, and his voice was heard, although rather softly, among the general chorus of Symbolists. But reading the poems of Vladimir Bestuzhev arouses an annoying feeling, as if you had recognized something good too late, when it is no longer needed.

The primary and indisputable merit of Vladimir Bestuzhev's poems lies in there melodious quality. The transition of vowels, the acceleration and retardation of rhythm, seem to fascinate the poet most of all, and he pays absolutely no attention to anything else. We will try, for example, to analyze the following poem, one of the best in the book:

> You hear—as in a cold river
> The soundless water sing—
> It runs in a free stream
> And will never tire.
> And we, when at evening-time
> The sky will just grow dim,
> Depart for eternal peace—
> And silence and peaceful sleep;

And drowsily and sweetly
Sings the soundless water—
That the night-time sleep, that the short dusk is
Not forever, not forever...

If one separates the concept of the river from the concept of the water, the epithet "cold" can be applied only to the latter; the epithet "free" in relation to the word "stream" says nothing to our imagination; just as useless is the information that the water "will never tire," because no one even thinks of doubting this. Then, in the second stanza the repeated form of the predicate proves that the subject is sleep, while by "eternal peace" it is customary to understand death. The word "silence" is devoid of strength and meaning (let us recall, for example, Edgar Allan Poe's "Silence"[3]), because what kind of silence is this, if one can hear the water sing? "The short dusk is not forever" is a pleonasm. Four *and*'s in a row in two lines (the eighth and ninth) are unpleasant to the ear. And after all, very little is said in the whole poem. All these mistakes are also characteristic of other poems by Vladimir Bestuzhev. Striving to conceal the poverty of thought and image with pomposity of themes and expressions composed of incorrectly used clichés, these poems nonetheless "sing" and therefore cannot be dismissed from poetry.

Apollo, No. 9, 1912.

XXVIII

Boris Gurevich. *The Eternally Human: Book of Cosmic Poetry.* **SPb. 2 R.**
Alexander Tinyakov (Odinoky). *Navis Nigra: Book of Poems.* **Moscow: Grif, 1912. 75 k.**
Nikolai Zhivotov. *Southern Flowers: Poems.* **Book Two. 1912.**

In our contemporary literary epoch, when Symbolism has penetrated the crowd and ceased to satisfy the pious craving for something new, crowds of Modernists have appeared, making a fuss and clamor and dreaming of reigning, if only for one day. Grigory Novitsky, and after him the Ego-Futurists, issued manifestoes that surpassed even the placards of provincial cinematographers in their grandiloquent illiteracy. From this crowd, one ought to single out Boris Gurevich (though by no means for his manifestos and poems), because he is sincerely carried away by his own theories, and his ignorance is learned ignorance. The doctrine of "scientism" that he is working out is only a vulgarization of the ideas of René Ghil, which have already shown themselves to be unsound. In pursuit of themes taken from the realm of science, Boris Gurevich has in mind not the living, divinely enigmatic contemporary man, but some sort of abstract, average one, for whom the poet proves to be Dante, having substituted knowledge of the exact sciences for the perception of God. Of course, such a dream is only a vestige of the passion for positivism in the Sixties and Seventies of the last century, but it is characteristic that even the imitators of Nihilism hope to achieve a revolution in art. Is it possible there was nothing in Symbolism that would sound to them like "hands off"? Boris Gurevich deserves no more attention as a poet than as a theoretician. His poems are unoriginal, slack, verbose and not infrequently illiterate.

The good poems of the talented Alexander Tinyakov (Odinoky), well-known to the readers of *Scales, The Crossing* and *Apollo*, lose much in a book. Before, it seemed that they were on the periphery of the poet's work, that they were only variations on some others, unread, fully encompassing his dream; now we see that there is no such dream, and that their glitter is not the glitter of diamonds, but of glass.

The most important quality in them is that of the themes (not, however, those inevitable ones that grow up from the depths of the spirit, but the accidental ones discovered elsewhere). Therefore you feel the poems themselves to be the usual children of days past. Alexander Tinyakov is a student of Bryusov, but how right was Andrei Bely in saying that Bryusov's armor crushes the sickly intellectuals who desire to put it on. Tinyakov is one of those who have been crushed.

Nikolai Zhivotov's first book, *Ragged Nerves*, caught the interest of many people with the boldness of invention and a certain strength that show through the unusually careless execution. Hopes were placed on him as a poet capable of achieving considerable eminence through persistent labor. Nikolai Zhivitov did not justify these hopes; *Southern Flowers* is proof of this. We all know that refined taste is a very loose concept and in any case is not the most valuable quality in a poet, but a total lack of taste makes Nikolai Zhivotov's book completely unacceptable. It robs his thoughts of all inspiration and literally covers his images with the ulcers of leprosy. Never before, it seems, have I had to read a cruder book of poetry.

Apollo, No. 10, 1912.

XXIX

Vyacheslav Ivanov. *Tender Secret:* Λεπτά. SPb.: Ory, 1912. —Vadim Gardner. *From Life to Life.* Moscow: Al'tsiona. —Alexei Skaldin. *Poems.* SPb.: Ory. —Sergei Solovyov. *Princess's Flower Bed: Third Book of Poems (1910-1912).* Moscow: Musaget, 1913. —Alexander Roslavlev. *Pipe.* SPb.: Soyuz. —Yakov Lyubyar. Contra-*dictions.* (3 Vols.) SPb. —Vsevolod Kurdyumov. *Powdered Heart.* SPb. —Vadim Shershenevich. *Carmina.* Moscow.

Many poets have stood among the ranks of the Symbolists, many were proud to bear this name, but at the present time only two have remained with the standard; the keys of Russian Symbolism are entrusted to only two. These two are Vyacheslav Ivanov and Fyodor Sologub.

Vyacheslav Ivanov is a young poet, that is, one who is far from having completed all phases of his development, but these phases have ceased to be significant for Russian poetry, they are necessary and pleasurable only to the poet himself. For others, he still has the same slogans, undoubtedly true, but, alas, well-known.

> ...Who has spurned the stage of the Dove
> Is named for creeping Serpents...
> ...As two-faced as the soul of a magnet,
> Passion of Flesh is fused with the Grave,
> With Birth, Sorrow.

And, finally, as his greatest perception:

> ...the Secret is tender.

It is perfectly obvious that it is not a matter of slogans, but of emotional content and the entire case of mind which accompanies it. Really, one must admit that in no other book has Vyacheslav Ivanov risen to such heights. His verse has acquired the strength of confidence and impetuosity, his images—precision and color, his composition—clarity and beautiful simplicity. On every page, you feel that you are dealing with a great poet who has reached the full development of his powers. But how far this individual, solitary development is from that balance of all the capacities of the spirit, which many dream of now.... Between Vyacheslav Ivanov and Acmeism, there is a gulf which no talent can fill....

Vadim Gardner,[1] despite all the inexperience which distinguishes young poets, has written a charming book of light verse. Of course, there is still the question whether this is not merely a seeming lightness, but Vadim Gardner does not ask himself this question. He fully believed the words of his muse:

> You are dear to me because, from tender, serene childhood
> Devoted to flowers and dream, you were friends with the streams.

But bashful reverie hides many dangers for the poet. Gardner did not avoid a single one of them. At times he is insipid, at times sickly-sweet, at times grandiloquent, and most often, impertinent. And it is terrible for a talented poet to remain a dilettant forever.

In his poems, Alexei Skaldin[2] is Vyacheslav Ivanov's double, a poor, shabby double. He selects rhythms, images and themes from the master diligently and joylessly and stacks them up like some sort of blocks. This is not an apprenticeship, which is sometimes so useful. A real student always comes to the teacher with his own content, and in his apparent humility one can always see the fervor of future emancipation. The weak will and sluggishness of Alexei Skaldin's poems are a bad sign. There is nothing in the book (not to count his imitative ability) that would make you believe in him as a poet. But he is not a bad versifier, and he discovered something in Vyacheslav Ivanov's *laboratory*.

There are two great shortcomings in Sergei Solovyov's poems:[3] they are contrived and for that reason not diversified; and this contrivance grew out of a very meager fantasy. Sergei Solovyov is obsessed by schemes: first he investigates the history of his race and dreams of creating a synthesis from the confusion of cultures and classes, then, in an utterly scholastic manner, he reduces the new Russian culture to three sources and also hopes to deduce from this the future Russian Renaissance. Is not such striving to summarize everything at any price by means of a mathematically exact formula evidence that the poet repudiates the significance of our times and does not trust the future at all? For this is that same notorious mystical anarchism, belief in the imminent end of the world. Hence the results for poetry are very sad: either exercises on historical and mythological themes, or a clumsy affectations of naivete "in the style of" old poets. With his new book Sergei Solovyov, a talented poet and the author of many beautiful stanzas and poems, disappoints those who believe in him.

Alexander Roslavlev ceased being considered among the ranks of poets long ago. About six or seven years ago people placed some hopes in him, and thought that, having passed his period of apprenticeship, he would find himself. But it soon became clear that this apprenticeship was only a crude and incoherent seizure of other people's devices, themes, ideas, experiences. That is how things stand now. Alexander Roslavlev's new books, lacking the freshness of a beginning, are frightening in their "poetisimilitude." *Pipe* is notable only in that there are more bad poems.

Yakov Lyubyar,[4] making his sudden debut with three books, is more verbose than befits a poet. For the joy of poetry lies precisely in saying in one or two lines what would take a prose writer a whole page. Yakov Lyubyar does not know this, just as he does not know most of the most elementary rules of versification.   In sometimes melodious, more often clumsy verses, he shamelessly tells everything he thinks and feels. Fortunately for him and for the reader, these thoughts are astute and often quite serious, the feelings deep and original.   The lack of imitation makes the book even more interesting.   One would like Yakov Lyubyar to master the technique of poetry a bit faster and become a real poet, and not just an alluring promise.

Vsevolod Kurdyumov's *Powdered Heart* is one of the most unpleasant books of the season, because it is so extremely characteristic of that reckless esthetic snobbery which has recently found more and more followers and admirers. Its casual treatment of the Russian language does not even attempt to hide behind the flag of one of the new schools, which have made some often very risky attempts in this direction. As in the first book, there are actors' tricks "near the end of the act." Where the poet tries to imitate Kuzmin, his clumsiness reaches an extreme. And strangest of all, they are contemporary, these poems, they are accessible, and should appeal to movie-goers, benighted gymnasts and...those who stroll on Nevsky around eleven o'clock at night. But does literature really exist for "them"?

Vadim Shershenevich's book produces a beautiful impression. The well-made verse (the rare irregularities are scarcely felt), the unpretentious but uniform style, the interesting constructions create delight in his poems. He knows how to turn a stanza and not fall under its power. His refined rhymes do not outweigh the lines. He is a student of Alexander Blok—sometimes more submissive than one would like—in his eidolology (the system of images). But a striving toward clarity and understanding is already perceptible in his poems, as a revolt against the mood of early German Romanticism in Russian poetry. It seems to me that taking this path, he may realize many of the valuable things that already glimmer in *Carmina*. And perhaps only then will he free himself from the antiquated literary tone that sometimes makes his best poems grow cold.

Apollo, No. 3, 1913.

XXX

Hatchery of Judges II. **SPb.: Zhuravl.**

The circle of writers[1] who joined together for the publication of this collection automatically inspires confidence, both by its undoubted revolutionary character in the area of the word, and by the absence of petty hooliganism. It devotes its main attention to review of stylistic problems and strives to restore to the word that strength and freshness which it lost through long use. Unfortunately, the demands of rhythmics and composition are lost sight of in the pursuit of style; the works therefore do not have that wholesomeness which would make them significant.

The selection of authors is not entirely successful. Vladimir Mayakovksy has much in common with the Ego-Futurists. Elena Guro[2] approaches Boris Zaitsev and the neo-Impressionists. Benedikt Livshits's[3] tawdry prettiness is sometimes unpleasant. Vladimir Khlebnikov[4] and Nikolai Burlyuk[5] can be singled out as the most interesting and powerful.

The Hyperborean, February, 1913.

XXXI

Valery Bryusov. *Nellie's Poems.* **Moscow: Skorpion, 1913. —Igor Severyanin.** *Seething Goblet of Thunder: Poèsies.* **Moscow: Grif, 1913. —Velimir Khlebnikov. —Osip Mandelstam.** *Stone: Poems.* **SPb.: Akme, 1913. —Count Vasily Alexeevich Komarovsky.** *First Landing: Poems.* **SPb.: Golike and Vilborg, 1913. —Innokenty Annensky.** *Famira Kifared: A Bacchic Drama.* **Posthumous publication. Moscow: V.P. Portugalov, 1913. —Fyodor Sologub.** *Collected Poems.* **Vol 13.** *Pearly Luminaries: Poems.* **SPb.: Sirin, 1913.**

A book has been published at the Skorpion Press which seems mysterious at first glance—*Nellie's Poems*, with a dedication to Valery Bryusov.[1] *Nellie* is an indeclinable word, and you do not know if it is in the genitive or dative case. One critic even thought that these are Bryusov's poems, but the latter disavowed them in a letter to the editor.

The poetic exploit of this book—every book of poems has its exploit—is profoundly and originally conceived: every image—it does not matter whether of dream or reality—is to be perceived with hallucinating clarity, to be felt at its absolute value, not ethical but esthetic. A weakness for material culture makes the poet forget the difference between the temporal and the eternal, for he wants to perceive both time and eternity as an instant. The circle of a glade is the same for him as a Persian carpet, the blue dragon-flies are like little monoplanes. What difference does it make to him that dragon-flies were flitting about not only when there was no man, or that the circle of a glade will see the ruin of all things living or made by human hand, —he loves life and not the world, caprice and the mistakes of his consciousness, and not the laws of existence of objects. He is only vaguely aware of this existence, people and things for him are no more significant and effective than abstractions. He does not embrace woman, but a "strange rapture," and he cherishes a "burst of passion" in cold hands. When I read these lines, I automatically recall the traditional image of the mother rocking a doll or a log in place of a dead child....

But a great, irremediable mistake lies at the bottom of every tragic fate, and the poet recognizes it, bitterly crying: "Your magic swells like empty window-dressing..." And on almost ever page of this book, one senses a door to another real world, where it is so good to escape from the imprudently cherished and unleashed nightmares of the everyday: from the Caucasian ottoman, the count from "El Dorado," the glass of irrua.... The poet changes from a reporter into the creator of true reality, true because it is always being created, into Shakespeare's Prospero:

> There palms toss obediently,
> Streams noiselessly murmur;
> There zebras with patterned skin,
> Raise the sands with their hoofs.
> There angels, lowering their wings
> To prostrate themselves before the Lord,
> Look at giant elephants,
> At little whimsical birds.
> There eternal Adam, awakened
> From a strange, sweet dream,
> Looks at Eve, astounded,
> And their conversation is silence....

Nellie's Poems reminds me of Hoffmann's Golden Vase.[2] Just as in that work all the effects were built on the contrast between the bourgeois life of a German town and the fiery images of Eastern legends, so here the snobbish admiration for the beauties of city life is compared with the magnificence of the creations of "Eternal Adam," awakened from a dream. The only thing one can hold against the Russian poet is the lack of connection between these two themes: they in no way proceed one from the other, and the poet, tempted by the desire to give everything a decisive blessing, instead of a firm, manly "yes" and "no," gives both an indecisive "yes."

Much has already been written and said about *Seething Gob-*

let of Thunder, the poèsies of Igor Severyanin. Sologub gave it a very unconstrained foreword, Bryusov praised it in *Russian Thought*,[3] where one would expect it to be condemned.

Indeed, the book is a highly characteristic one, really a cultural event. Russian society has already long since split into men of books and men of newspapers, who have almost no point of contact between each other. The first lived in a world of millenial images and ideas, spoke little, knowing what responsibility one must bear for each word, examined their feelings, afraid to betray the idea, loved like Dante, died like Socrates, and, according to the others, probably resembled badgers.... The others, brisk and bustling, forced their way into the very thick of contemporary life, read the evening papers, spoke of love with their barber and of brilliantine with their beloved, used only ready-made phrases or some sort of intimate little words, the hearing of which brought out a certain feeling of awkwardness in the uninitiated. The first were shaved by the others, ordered boots from them, dealt with them through official papers, or gave them promissory notes, but never thought about them and would by no means name them. In short, relations were the same as between the Romans and the Germans on the eve of the great migrations.

And suddenly—oh, this "suddenly" is really indispensable here—the neo-Romans, the men of books, heard the youthfully ringing and powerful voice of a real poet, speaking in the Volapuk[4] of newspaper men about the "bases" of their strange existence, unknown until now. Igor Severyanin is really a poet and what is more, a new poet. That he is a poet is proven by the wealth of his rhythms, the abundance of images, the soundness of composition, and his own keenly-experienced themes. He is new in that he, before all other poets, insisted on the poet's right to be candid to the point of vulgarity.

I hasten to make a reservation. His vulgarity appears such only for the men of books. When he wishes to "fervently glorify the Reichstag and the Bastille, the courtesan and the schematist,[5] impetuosity and dream," the men of newspapers see nothing unnatural in it. They read about the Reichstag daily, have acquaintance with courtesans, and readily speak of impetuosity and dream, riding bicycles with the young ladies. For Severyanin, Goethe is glorious not in himself, but thanks to (imagine!) Ambroise Thomas,[6] whom he even calls "the glorifier of Goethe." For him, Pushkin "became Derzhavin,"[7] and at the same time, he himself is "the

131

genius Igor Severyanin." Well, maybe he is right. Pushkin is not printed in handbills; Goethe in pure form is scarcely intelligible to the provincial stage. Even if one hears the firm voice of Kozma Prutkov,[8] for men of newspapers, even Kozma Prutkov is not at all comical; it is not without reason that one of them took "Vampuka" seriously.

We are also already acquainted with another side of Igor Severyanin. How could one not recognize the schoolgirl joy of Apukhtin's "letters" in these lines, for example:

> It cannot be, you are lying to me, dreams!
> You could not forget me in separation...
> I remember when, in a surge of torment,
> You wanted to burn my letters...burn them!...you!...

or these:

> ...The Child was dying. The mother, writing.
> And you, like a mother, responded to the voice of torment,
> Forgetting that to neither art nor science
> Is given the power to steal from death.

But again, the poet is right: such poems move many to tears, and it is not important that they stand outside art in their cheap theatricality. That was why universal Ego-Futurism was founded, to widen the boundaries of art...

I repeat, all this is very serious. We are witnessing a new invasion of barbarians, powerful in their talent and terrible in their indelicacy. Only the future will show whether these are "Germans" or...Huns, of whom not a trace will remain.

Viktor Khlebnikov has still not published his poems in a separate book. But he has contributed a great deal to the publications *Hylaea*,[9] *Studio of the Impressionists*[10] and so forth, so one can already speak of him as a fully formed poet. His work falls into three parts: theoretical investigations along with illustrations, into the area of style, poetic work and comic verses. Unfortunately, the boundaries between them are extremely carelessly drawn, and often a fine poem is ruined by the admixture of an unexpected and clumsy joke or by far from well-considered word formations.

Keenly sensitive to word roots, Viktor Khlebnikov deliberately ignores inflections, sometimes discarding them completely, sometimes changing them beyond recognition. He believes that each vowel contains within itself not only action but its direction: thus *bik* (bull) is that which strikes, *bok* (side) is that which is stricken; *bobr* (beaver) is that which is hunted, *babr* (tiger) is that which hunts, etc.

Taking the root of the word and adding arbitrary inflections, he creates new words. Thus, from the root *sme* (laugh), he creates *"smekhagi"* ("laughomanes" or "laughletes"), *"smeevo"* ("laugh-ishly"), *"smeyungiki"* ("laugherasters"), *"smeyanstvovat'"* (laugh-erate"), etc.[11] He dreams of the simplest language, made only of prepositions, which would indicate the direction of motion. Those of his poems like *"Smekhagi," "Pereverten'"* and *"Chyornii Lyu-bir',"* are, to a significant extent, the dictionary for such a "pos-sible" language.

As a poet, Viktor Khlebnikov loves nature in a conjuring manner. He is never satisfied with what is. His deer changes into a carnivorous beast; at the "private viewing,"[12] he sees the dead birds on the ladies' hats come to life, the clothes fall off the people and transform—the woolens into a sheep, the linens into little blue flax flowers.

He loves and knows how to speak of remote times, to make use of their images. For example, his primeval man tells us:

> ...What was with me
> Just now?
> Beast, with a howl barking
> (Terrible leap,
> Hot breath),
> Face burn.
> What a death!
> Wild breath,
> Eyes glittering,
> Huge snout...
> But my knife saved,
> Or I die.
> This time
> Was trace bruise.

Both in the rhythms and in the tangled syntax you see the frightened savage, hear his agitated words...

A somewhat naive chauvinism contributed much of value to

Khlebnikov's poetry. He perceives Russia as an Asian land (although he does not ask her to learn wisdom from the Tatars), affirms her distinctiveness and struggles with European trends. Many of his lines seem like snatches from some great, never-recorded epos:

> Joking, in a flock, we scratch
> The water father's heels with a laugh.
> His simple family
> Was with us at Christmas-tide.

Weakest of all are his jokes, which create an impression not of laughter but of convulsions. But he jokes often and always inappropriately. When Juno's lover calls her "auntie dear," when someone says, "my jaw dropped from delight," it is sad for a poet.

In general, Viktor Khlebnikov has found his path, and by following it he can become an important poet. So much the worse to see what a commotion they have raised over his work, how they borrow not his achievements but his failures, of which there are, alas, too many. He must learn a great deal more, if only from himself, and those who inflate his still unfirmed talent, risk its eventual bursting.

Osip Mandelstam's *Stone* is the poet's first book, published some time ago. There are poems in it dated 1909. Despite that, there are only two dozen poems in all. This is explained by the fact that the poet moved relatively recently from the Symbolist to the Acmeist camp, and regards his earlier poems with increased severity, selecting only those that are really valuable. Thus, his book falls into two sharply distinguished sections: before 1912, and after.

In the first, there are the usual Symbolist virtues and shortcomings, but even here the poet is strong and original. The delicacy of fully regulated rhythms, a sense of style, a somewhat lace-like composition, are present in full measure even in his first poems. In these poems, the weariness, pessimism and disillusionment characteristic of all young poets, which in others produces only unnecessary tests of the pen, crystallize for Osip Mandelstam in the poetic idea-image: in Music with a capital M. He is willing to give up the world for the sake of Music:

134

Remain as foam, Aphrodite,
And word, revert to music...

renounce nature—

And above the darkening wood
Stood the brazen moon;
Why so little music
And such silence?

and even poetry—

Why is the soul so melodious,
And why are there so few sweet names,
And why is the instantaneous rhythm only chance,
Unexpected Aquilo?[13]

But a poet cannot live long on a denial of the world, and a poet with burning heart and spirited love will not want images which you cannot look at, and which you cannot touch with a caressing hand. Already on page 14 of his book, Osip Mandestam makes an important admission: "No, not the moon, but a bright clock-face shines at me..." With this, he opened the doors of his poetry to all the phenomena of life, to those living in time, and not just in eternity or an instant: to the casino on the dunes, the parade at Tsarskoe Selo, the restaurant rabble, a Lutheran's funeral. With purely southern passion, he grew to love northern decorum and even simply the austerity of ordinary life. He is in ecstasy over that "secret fear" which "the coach, returning home with the relics of a gray-haired fraulein," inspires in him: with the very same love, he loves "the jurist, with a sweeping gesture drawing his greatcoat about him," and Russia, which, "monstrous—like a battleship in dock—rests heavy." At the Lutheran's funeral, what he liked most of all what that "there was a look clouded with a seemly tear, and the bells rang with restraint." I do not remember anyone who could so completely destroy the romantic in himself and not affect the poet at the same time.

This very love for everything alive and durable leads Osip Mandelstam to architecture. He loves buildings just as other poets love mountains or the sea. He describes them in detail, finds parallels between them and himself, and on the basis of their lines constructs universal theories. It seems to me that this is the most successful approach to the now fashionable problem of urbanism.

Mandelstam's Symbolist passions are ended forever, and these lines sound as their epitaph:

> And far better than the ravings
> Of an inflamed mind are
> Stars, sober conversation,
> The west wind off the Neva.

Until now, I have found only one review, superficial and hostile, of *First Landing,* a book of poems by Count Vasily Komarovsky,[14] which came out at the beginning of autumn. The book was obviously not a success, and that raises some bitter thoughts. How could our critics, so indiscriminately tolerant of everything, celebrating all the anniversaries, encouraging all innovations, so concertedly turn away from this, a book not of promises (so many of them have not been fulfilled), but of the accomplishments of an undeniable poet's decade of creative labor?

Count Vasily Komarovsky does not force us to follow this labor. At most, six or seven early, weak poems show us what path he took to reach the depth and significance of his present thought and form. All the poems since 1909 are already the poems of a master, although scarcely those of a teacher. Count Komarovsky, in all probability, will never be a teacher, the very character of his work, solitary and spare, preventing him. Beneath many of the poems, there is the inscription "Tsarskoe Selo," beneath others, it can be surmised. And from this, much can be inferred. The poet was carried away by a little town, lost amid huge parks with columns, arches, palaces, pavilions and swans on clear lakes, a town illuminated by the memory of Pushkin, Zhukovsky, and in recent times, Innokenty Annensky, and he gave us not only the special landscape of Tsarskoe Selo, but Tsarskoe Selo's sphere of ideas.

> Where the bronze visages of Tiberius and Sulla
> Remind me of gloomy debauches,
> With the last scent of the last mignonette,
> The heavy autumn smoke entered all the gardens,
> Dulled everywhere the gilded patches of light,
> And the black swans' frightened cries
> By the grey shores, revealed thin ice
> On the fresh tremor of the dark lilac waters...

136

Reading these lines, you remember, and remember with pleasure, Henri de Régnier[15] and Innokenty Annensky. Kinship of
spirit is still not apprenticeship. And the very idea, so brilliantly
realized—of fusing the French poet's esthetic power of observation
with the Russian's tense lyricism—indicates Count Komarovsky's
creative independence. Besides that, there is in his poems a love
for Byzantium, or rather for the idea of Byzantium, strong, little
revealed as yet, but possessed of the power to enchant. He is of
course speaking of this in these lines:

> ...The Mother slept. Where in avid flight
> Dreams flew to the marriage cypress—
> She streamed in the Seven-citied Kingdom
> In the yawning dark and icy rizas![16]

The lyric-landscape poems are compiled together in the first
section; they are very "Tsarsko-selian," although sometimes ascribed
to other places at the author's caprice.

The second section contains the lyric-epic poems, a light-
hearted excursion through centuries and countries. Rome in three
sonnets, Byzantium again, the Renaissance, and the charming
"Maidservant's Song," naturally, a German maid, with her post-
man on a high coachbox, Fichte[17] and Monsieur le baron. In these
poems, one enjoys the fervor and the exact, although scarcely ar-
cheological, knowledge of the details of everyday life.

The third section—"Impressions of Italy"—is less significant
than the preceding ones, although perhaps more perfect with respect to rhythm.

The two translations in the fourth section—of Baudelaire's
"Le Voyage" and Keats' well-known "Ode to a Grecian Urn"[18]—
are very inexact and suffer from a certain syntactic disorder, although they are done with great élan.

Innokenty Annensky's bacchic drama, *Famira Kifared*, which
came out this year in an edition of one hundred numbered copies,
is, after *The Cypress Chest,* the deceased poet's most significant
book. It is a continuation and completion of his earlier attempts
to revive antiquity, like *Ixion, Melannippe the Philosopher, Laodamia*[19] and the treatise "The Ancient World in Contemporary
French Poetry," important for the depth and novelty of the ideas
expressed in it. Innokenty Annensky, all impulse, all trembling,

was equally far from both the Renaissance idea that the world is not ahead of, but behind us, that is, with the ancient Greeks, and from the contemporary desire to pillage that strange and beautiful world, using ready-made thoughts and sonorous proper names. He has a deep feeling for myth, as a situation existing from the beginning of time, or rather, as a relation between two intransient unities, that is only very superficially connected with the epoch that discovered it. Only good taste and a striving toward the beautiful difficulty (he speaks of this, by the way, in the above-mentioned treatise) prevented him from creating symbolic-allegorical dramas within a mythical framework. Not for anything did he want to abandon the present, with its vivid, graphic language and psychological nuances, for the sake of dismal abstraction; but in treating myth a touch of the unusual was indispensable, and he achieved it, capriciously combining the ancient with the contemporary. His characters are taken from the ancient world; they do nothing that would be uncharacteristic for their epoch, but their conversations, with the exception of the general poetic intensification (the drama was written in 1906), are strikingly contemporary. Of course, we do not know how the ancient Greeks spoke, the language of their poets is not conversational language, but still, it is impossible to believe that echoes of Balmont and Verlaine could be heard in their words. Innokenty Annensky does this quite consciously, almost as though with defiance, as is shown by such anachronisms as Apollo's famous violin. In *Famira Kifared,* there are two musical motives, separate, but indispensable to each other: the story of Famira and the background against which it is played out, the choruses now crazed maenades, now jovial satyrs. This is the framework of the story: "Famira or Famirid, the son of the Thracian king Philammon and the nymph Argiope, was renowned for playing the cithara; his arrogance reached the point that he challenged the Muses to a contest, but was defeated, and as punishment, deprived of sight and the gift of music." Annensky complicates this scheme with the nymph's unexpected love for her son, and portrays him as a dreamer, for whom love is alien, but who still perishes in the net of the woman in love with him.[20] Fate appears in the image of the splendidly indifferent muse, Euterpe,[21] of whom one of the characters says:

> Haughty—when she passes among us,
> She gathers up her dress with her hand. Fingers—

138

And rings are beautiful on her pink
And slender fingers—only, I suppose, her hands
Are cold—and she is always looking at them
With a smile—she is so content...

Famira burns out his eyes with coals and goes off to beg alms;
the guilty mother, transformed into a bird, accompanies him in his
wanderings and draws lots from the useless cithara. They set off,
as if they had hangovers, and behind, the exultant and languorous
call of the maenades still sounds, even more audible in memory:

> Evoe, O god, they broke our circle,[22]
>   O Dionysius!
> You see, how, languorously spent, hung
> The hoop of hot, of white hands,
>   O Dionysius!

Fyodor Sologub's *Pearly Luminaries*, the thirteenth volume
of his collected works, includes selected poems from thirty years
of poetic work. For the literary historian they will be an invalu-
able aid, so fully, so clearly do they reflect all the changes in device, mood and theme in Russian poetry. Here is the somewhat
sickly-sweet lucidity of the eighties, and the shy estheticism of the
nineties, then the justification of evil, politics, a searching for God,
questions of sex and, finally, the gently irony of a sage of this
world. As a great poet, Sologub is very sensitive to the moods of
the crowd, and while not adapting himself to it at all, lives at the
same pace, which explains his fully deserved popularity. Besides
that, he is an innovator, and if that often prevents his poems from
being contemporary, they gain in the pungency with which they
strike the heart.

There are a few new poems in this book which will always remain in the most exacting, the most selective anthologies of Russian
poetry: "Joseph's Beauty," "Again the nighttime silence," "My
bright house ever higher" and "Dull Green of the Olives" are the
most important.

Apollo, No. 1-2, 1914.

XXXII

Sergei Gorodetsky. *Flowering Staff.* SPb.: Gryadushchy den'. 1 R.
Anna Akhmatova. *Rosary.* SPb.: Giperborei, 1914. 1 R 25 k.
Pavel Radimov. *Earthly Raiment.* Kazan': 1914. 1 R.
Georgy Ivanov. *Chamber.* SPb.: Giperborei, 1914.
Vladislav Khodasevich. *Happy Home.* Moscow: Altsiona, 1914.
Jean Chuzeville. *Anthologie des poètes russes.* Paris: éd. Crès.

The turning point in Sergei Gorodetsky's work is *Flowering Staff.* Possessing an inexhaustible melodic power (and in this regard, comparable only with Balmont), bearing a cheerful and light-winged spirit, which is readily daring and does not ponder over its expressions, in short, the curly-headed singer of Russian song, he finally found a means for the definition of his potential, certain norms which developed and strengthened his talent. True, owing to this, his earlier image is lost, the image of the merry-maker and eccentric, "who runs his fingers over the strings," sometimes of a gusli, more often of a balalaika. Now we can expect from his works a soundness and beauty attainable only by the combination of three conditions: deep unconscious impulses, a strict understanding of them, and a powerful will in their realization.

This is mentioned in the author's preface to the collection: "...being an Acmeist, I was as much as possible simple, direct and honest in treating the relations between the object and the word, obscured by Symbolism and unusually fragile by nature. I wanted to use absolutely no exaggeration, or extended commentary, or high-flown interpretation. And because of that, the world lost none of its marvelous complexity, it did not become trivial."

Flowering Staff consists wholly of octaves, forms first worked out in France by Moréas.[1] It is convenient, since it gives the poet the opportunity to record the most fleeting thoughts and feelings, which would never crystallize into a real poem. A collection of such "octets" gives the impression of a very unconstrained diary, and behind it, it is so easy to see the face of the poet himself, to hear the intonation of his voice.

True, his task could have been dealt with in another way: many ideas have antipodes, so antithetical that you do not even guess the possibility of a synthesis. Their opposition in two stanzas of an octet would produce one of the most vivid poetic effects—surprise. But for that, it would have been necessary to reveal the

140

complex paradoxes of consciousness, to again perceive the world as dangerous and slightly hostile, and Sergei Gorodetsky has already found the means to give his blessing to everything; this active admiration is the finest discovery of the young century.

> Lord, how much beauty
> In Your omnicelestial world...

he cries, but as an Acmeist, he depicts not the beautiful, but his sensation of it. For what is beautiful in and of itself, or what can never be beautiful? The esthetes' mistake is that they search for the basis of joyful admiration in the object and not in the subject. Horror, pain, shame are beautiful and precious because they are so inseparably tied to the omnicelestial world and to our creative mastery of everything. When you live life as a lover, in the moment of the embrace you do not distinguish where pain stops and joy begins, you know only that you do not want another.

> How damned beloved life is,
> What bitter wine
> Is given me in a cup of hammered gold
> By a beautiful hand!
> But I drink, not knowing temptation:
> Will the beast of non-existence really
> Hold out to me in its ugly paw
> A ladle of the honey drink?

"What!" many will cry, "the poet renounces faith in the future life, with heavenly tabernacles, angels and immortality?" Yes, I answer, and he is a true poet: heavenly tabernacles are given to him here on earth, he feels the presence of angels in moments of inspired labor, and immortality...only poets, and perhaps their most attentive readers, know how flexible our conception of time is and what wonders it conceals for those able to control it! Annensky said that "infinity is only an instant, split by the lightning of torment." Eternity and an instant—these are not temporal concepts and therefore can be perceived in any interval; everything depends on the synthesizing progression of contemplation.

Everything is on earth and everything is accessible to man:

> O, beautiful pines, O, peals of summer lightning,
> Serve supper to the brethren!

Bring, Sirens, the amber keys
To the red-gold gates.

There are many shortcomings in *Flowering Staff*, perhaps even more than permissible in our day for a book by a well-known poet. Sergei Gorodetsky more often tells than shows, there are some very unfinished octets, there are even completely frivolous ones; there are rhythmic defects—an iambic hexameter without a caesura after the third foot, the same iambic hexameter which wormed its way into pentameters; the general cliches of Modernism are not infrequent. But the feelings that created this book are new and triumphant, and in regard to eidolology, it is a valuable and extremely timely contribution to poetry.

In Anna Akhmatova's *Rosary*, on the contrary, the eidolological aspect is thought out least of all. The poetess has not "created herself," has not put some sort of external fact in the center of her experiences in order to unify them; she does not address herself to something known or understandable to herself alone, and in this she is unlike the Symbolists; but on the other hand, her themes are often not exhausted by the limits of a given poem, much in them seems insubstantial because it is not fully proven. As with most young poets, in Anna Akhmatova one frequently finds the words pain, sorrow, and death. This youthful pessimism, so natural and therefore so beautiful, has been until now the property of "pen testers" and it seems that in Akhmatova's verse it has attained its place in poetry for the first time. I think everyone has wondered at the magnitude of youth's capacity and willingness to suffer. Laws and objects of the real world suddenly replace those former ones which have been pierced through by a dream in whose fulfillment he believed: the poet cannot help but see that they are in and of themselves incapable of comprehending himself among them, of coordinating the rhythm of his spirit with their rhythm. But the force of life and love is so powerful in him that he begins to love his orphanhood itself and achieves the beauty of pain and death. Later, when an "unexpected joy" begins to be revealed to his spirit, which is weary of always being in the same condition, he will feel that man can joyously comprehend all aspects of the world, and from the ugly duckling which he was in his own eyes

142

until then, he will become a swan, as in Anderson's fairy tale.

To people who are not fated to achieve such a transformation, or people who possess a feline memory which attaches itself to all passed stages of the spirit, Akhmatova's book will seem exciting and valuable. In it, a series of beings, mute until now, acquire a voice—women in love, cunning, dreamy and rapturous, at last speak their own genuine and at the same time artistically convincing language. That bond with the world which I spoke about earlier and which is the destiny of every genuine poet has almost been realized by Akhmatova, because she knows the joy of perceiving the external and knows how to transmit this joy to us.

> Tightly shut are her dry lips,
> Hot is the flame of three thousand candles.
> Thus Princess Eudoxia lay
> On sapphire, scented brocade.
>
> And, bent low, a mother tearlessly prayed
> For her blind little boy,
> And a hysterical woman thrashed voicelessly,
> Straining to gulp air with her lips.
>
> And from a southern land,
> A black-eyed humpbacked old man,
> As if at the gate of paradise
> Pressed close to the darkening step.

Here I turn to what is most significant in Akhmatova's poetry, her stylistics: she almost never explains, she shows. This is achieved by a carefully considered and original choice of images, but most important, by their detailed elaboration. Epithets defining the value of the object (such as beautiful, ugly, happy, unfortunate, etc.), occur rarely. This value is suggested by the description of an image and by the interrelationship of images. Akhmatova has many devices for this. I shall point out a few of them: the conjunction of an adjective defining color with an adjective defining form:

> ...And thickly the dark-green ivy
> Entwined the high window.

or:

> ...There, a raspberry sun
> Over dishevelled grey smoke...

Repetition in two successive lines, which doubles our attention to the image:

> ...Tell me how they kiss you,
> Tell me how you kiss them.

or:

> ...In snowy branches to black jackdaws
> To black jackdaws give shelter.

Transformation of an adjective into a noun:

> ...The orchestra is playing (something) gay...

and so forth.

There are many definitions of color in Akhmatova's verse, and most frequently, of yellow and gray, until now very rare in poetry. And perhaps as confirmation of the nonaccidental nature of her taste, most of the epithets emphasize that very poverty and paleness of objects: a threadbare rug, worn-down heels, a faded flag, etc. In order to love the worled, Akhmatova must see it as dear and simple.

Akhmatova's rhythmics are a great help to her stylistics. Paeons and pauses help her single out the most necessary words in a line, and in the whole book I did not find a single example of stress falling on an unstressed word, or, contrarily, of a word stressed in meaning without stress. If someone were to assume the task of examining a collection of any contemporary poet from this point of view, he would be convinced that usually the case is otherwise. A weakness and gasping for breath is characteristic of Akhmatova's rhythmics. The four-line stanza, in which almost the entire book is written, is too long for her. Her periods usually encompass two lines, sometimes three, sometimes only one. The causal relationship with which she attempts to replace the rhythmic unity of the stanza does not achieve, for the most part, its goal. The poetess must elaborate upon her stanza if she wishes to master composition. A single spontaneous impulse cannot serve as the basis for composition. This is why Akhmatova knows as yet only the sequence of a logically developed thought or the sequence by which objects fall into her field of vision. This does not constitute a shortcoming of her poems, but it blocks the path ahead of her for achieving much that is worthwhile.

In comparison with *Evening*, published two years ago, *Rosary* represents a great step forward. The verse has become more resolute, the content of each line more solid, the choice of words chastely spare and, best of all, the incoherence of thought, so characteristic of *Evening*, and comprising more of a psychological curiosity than a feature of poetry, has disappeared.

When Pavel Radimov's first book came out about two years ago, he put so much wild passion and unexpectedness in thematic approach into his *Field Psalms* that great hopes were immediately placed on the author. *Earthly Raiment* is disappointing: we can conclude from it that we are dealing with a poet who wished to mark off a small area for himself and not stick his nose out any farther. It was customary to call poets who voluntarily narrowed down their work, stylists. I would call them something more offensive, because it is just as if some evil fate moves them to choose, of all poses, the most sickly-sweet and affected. The pose in which Pavel Radimov chose to rigidify is the pose of a man bestowing his blessing upon the world. That is not so bad! What is bad is that for him the world is plastered with a thick coating of tinsel.

> ...The language of inspired nature,
> Wise and simple, is intelligible to me,
> And in my imperishable soul, I
> Merge wih eternal beauty...

he informs us, and so, completely gives himself away. The language of nature really is wise, but not at all simple, at least for human feeling, and the sensation we derive from the world can hardly fit into the concept of beauty. To synthesize in this way, one needs thunderous, Tyutchevian words which pierce the soul with blue lightning, but there are none in Radimov's vocabulary. He is much more enjoyable when he throws off the cardboard mask of sage, and, like a Realist, describes Bashkiria, village scenes and pictures of a bazaar. Here, his tenacious eye catches the necessary, along with the unnecessary, the vivid detail, the amusing analogy. And his descriptions are enlivened by a sly mockery that is purely Russian, even folklike. It is good to read his long poem in hexameters "Popiad," the story of a just-graduated seminarian, travelling with his father around the neighboring parishes to choose a bride for himself. It does not excite the reader for a minute, but throughout his reading he smells grass and lindens, hears dragonflies, church bells, and decorous turns of phrase with the letter o, and loves all these modest priests' daughters with light brown braids a fist thick:

> ...As dawn, rising to the golden heavens, plays
> Its bright smile of sunbeams on the green
> meadows and on the distant
> Wood, mysteriously blue, so Masha appeared to the guests,
> Arousing in Fyodor an exciting trembling with her charming form,
> And making Father Alexander, with lucid brow,
> Exclaim loudly: "Oh, your daughter is a queen, a princess!...

Realism has many ways of charming the soul, but there is nothing for it to say, nowhere for it to beckon.

> ...O, cat, wandering on the roof,
> Your dreams sing in me!...

...the author of *Chamber*, Georgy Ivanov, has attained self-definition. Like Akhmatova, he did not create himself, but rather the psychology of an idler who readily stops before a gaudily daubed poster and before a Negro in a red chlamys,[2] before an engraving and before a sensation, an idler, ready to merge with each rhythm he meets, to merge for a moment without any pleasure or curiosity—this psychology unites his poems. He does not think in images, I am very much afraid that he does not think at all. But he wants to talk about what he sees, and he likes the very art of speech. That is why his assonances sound like rhymes, his free meters like strictly metrical ones. For him, the world falls into a series of episodes, clear, charply outlined, and if sometimes complex, only in the manner of Ponson-du-Terrail.[3] Chinese dragons over the Neva strangle a chance passerby; a hunchback, husband of a music-hall singer, kills a Negro out of jealousy, a Finnish knife is hidden in a street punk's boot.... Of course, there is much naive romanticism in all this, but there is also the instinct of a contemplative person who, above all, desires a spectacle from life.

Georgy Ivanov's verse combines the dryness of epic and the energy of ballad. Here, for example, are excerpts from his poem "Fall Phantom":

> With desperate malice
> Distorting his face,
> Brandishing his cane,
> He came out on the roof...
> ...Splashing in the puddles,
> He strode down the streets,
> Hurled curses,
> One worse than the next...
> ...And he could have been a happy,
> Gay chatterer,
> And committed outrages over beer,
> Not knowing any other way.
> The fall wind in crude
> Flight rent the clouds,
> Cold rain ran
> Down the drainpipes.
> And he rushed with malice,
> Twisting his wet mustache,
> Stabbing at the puddles
> With his splintering cane.

One fears that Georgy Ivanov will grow tired of being just a poet and desire the greater scope of prose narration. But in that event, we must remember him as a talented adherent of entertaining poetry, the poetry of adventure, whose propagator in our literature was Vsevolod Krestovsky[4]—a rare tradition, but deserving of all possible attention, even if only because Zhukovsky was its prophet.

Vladislav Khodasevich's first book of poems came out in 1908, the second only now.[5] And after six years, he wanted to prepare only thirty-five poems. Such miserliness is very profitable for the poet. We do not grow accustomed to his dream or his intonation, he appears unexpectedly before us with interesting new words and does not stay too long, leaving behind him a pleasant feeling of not being fully satisfied and the desire for another visit. Both Tyutchev and

Annensky were like that,[6] and how they love them!

Khodasevich has the right to be such a nice guest. He is not dull; not dull to such an extent that he is not even paradoxical. When you do not agree with him and do not sympathize with him, you still believe and admire him. True, one would often like him to speak more confidently and to be freer in his gestures. A European in his love for the details of beauty, he is still a Slav in his sort of peculiar indifferent weariness and melancholy skepticism. Only hopes or sufferings can excite such a soul, and Khodasevich voluntarily, even with a certain arrogance, renounced both:

> Alas, child! Doesn't the insatiate soul
> Dream an inexpressible dream about you?
> Don't you come in the darkened shadow
> With a bouquet of roses, a dagger and wine?
> I watch sharply for your every step.
> You fall, you whisper—I sob,
> But I cannot make out the bitter words
> And do not understand the language of shadows.

In Khodasevich's poems, with their somewhat flaccid rhythmics and not always expressive stylistics, much attention is devoted to composition, and that is what makes them beautiful. The reader's attention follows the poet easily, as if in a graceful dance, now dying away, now gliding, going deeper, or rising along the lines, which end harmonically, and which are new for every poem. The poet is either unable or does not wish to use all this energy from the rhythmic motion of ideas and images to create the temple of a new world-perception; he is for now only a ballet-master, but the dances he teaches are sacred dances.

Jean Chuzeville, who published in Paris an *Anthology of Russian Poets* with his own translations, limited his task to the latest period of Russian poetry, from Vladimir Solovyov to Alexei N. Tolstoi.[7] Only one extremely annoying gap crept into the book: Sergei Gorodetsky is not present, and the role of representative of folk themes in Russian poetry is assigned to Alexei N. Tolstoi, who was dependent during the entire course of his brief poetic career on Gorodetsky.

But despite this slip, one must welcome the book not only as the first fully serious attempt to acquaint France with our poetry, but as an anthology which in its selection of names and works, has no equal in Russia. Each poet is introduced with an article, which, in an interesting and sufficiently careful manner, evaluates the characteristics of his work and his position in literature. And it is easy to become reconciled to the fact that Bryusov in translation begins to sound like Viele-Griffin,[8] or that Blok turned out very similar to Maeterlinck. The translator is a poet himself (his book of poems, *La route poudroyee*, came out several years ago), and there is nothing surprising in the fact that he captures the correspondence between foreign and native rhythms even when this correspondence is merely imaginary. One must be especially grateful to him for the boldness with which he replaces rhyme with assonance, striving to reproduce the image exactly and to express the peculiarities of speech. Reading this book,you feel that something has been added to your earlier conception of the poets, and you begin to believe the paradox that to fully understand any poet it is necessary to read him translated into all languages.

How fine Vyacheslav Ivanov's trumpets sound:

> Hier encore l'assaut des titans
> Ruait les colonnes guerrières
> Dont les larges flancs palpitants
> Craquaient sous l'essieu des tonnerres...[9]

or how astonishing Sologub's transmitted delicacy:

> Elisabeth, Elisabeth
>   Entends mon voeu!
> Je meurs, je meurs, Elisabeth,
>   Je suis en feu.
> Muette, hélas! ta voix, muette;
>   En vain je prie;
> Elle est bien loin, Elisabeth,
>   Dans sa patrie...[10]

and finally, the cunning of Mikhail Kuzmin:

> —"Julie, à quoi bon cet aveu?
> N'est-ce point assez qu'un tel feu
> Vous cause mille ardeurs maudites."
> —"Oui. Mais j'ai vu le camélia
> Qui, hier, au bal, vous rallia

Tel coup d'oeil. —Vous y Répondîtes!"
—"J'en jure, par tous mes aieux,
Que je n'en veux qu'à vos beaux yeux
Aveugles —Et fi d'Amanda!"[11]

The bibliography is extremely incomplete, and for some poets goes only to 1910. Valery Bryusov's foreword, concise and meaningful, while not giving the Russian reader anything new, beautifully explains to a foreigner the position of Russian poetry in its recent past. And Jean Chuzeville, who published an article on the latest Russian Poetry in *Mercure de France* (November 1, 1913),[12] which is interesting, but can be faulted for its extreme lack of information, thinks that this is already the past.

Apollo, No. 5, 1914.

XXXIII

Maria Levberg. *Sly Pilgrim.* Petrograd: 1915. 60 k.—Leonid Berman. *Relentless Retinue.* Petrograd: 1915.—Mikhail Dolinov. *Rainbow.* Petrograd: 1915. 75 k.—Alexander Korona. *Alladin's Lamp.* Petrograd. 1 R 25 k.—Chrolli. *Gingham.* Petrograd: 1915. 25 k. —Anatoly Puchkov. *Last Quarter of the Moon.* Petrograd: 1915. 1 R.—Tikhon Churilin. *Spring After Death.* Moscow: 1915.—Count Alexander Saltykov. *In Old Tracks.* Petrograd: 1915. 1 R 25 k.— Prince G. Gagarin. *Poems.* Petrograd: 1915.—Vladimir Prussak. *Flowers in the Dump.* Petrograd: 1915. 1 R.

Maria Levberg's poems[1] too often reveal the poetic inexperience of their author. They contain almost all the Modernist cliches, beginning with the self-portrayal as a visored night and ending with the Parisian cafes and restaurants and even flowers in champagne. The approximate rhymes in the sonnets, hexameters suddenly popping up among pentameters,—in short, this is not yet a book, but only the voice of the poet, announcing her existence.

However, one feels in many poems a genuinely poetic experience, only one which has not found its real expression. There is material for poetry here: energy combined with reverie, the ability to see and hear, and a certain austere and tranquil melancholy, that is not at all like grief.

150

...Once I went out of the house,
Without grown-ups, entirely alone.
I met gnomes
In a garden with many-colored flower-beds.

All with branches of black spruce,
And only one with a staff;
They laughed and sang,
And invited me to their house.

They laughed so ringingly,
As if they found it funny,
Funny that they had feigned
Cheerfulness for a very long time...

These and the last poems in the book show that Maria Levberg is beginning to learn mastery of her material with that conscious persistence and unconscious success, which only fall the lot of poets.

In his very attractively published book, Leonid Berman appears a much more contemporary poet.[2] He has his own disposition, skepticism in the use of the everyday turning to conscientiousness of the spirit on higher levels. There is nothing in the book that is completely bad, and a great many stanzas bring delight with their unexpectedness, precision and melodiousness. One is disturbed only by the absence of his own themes sufficiently vividly outlined, of significant experiences, and of the feeling of tragic doom toward art. The poet is content enough with an interesting simile, a successful epithet, a ringing line, to make a poem from this:

Often late on the Neva you
Pass with weary tread;
Melancholy, with indiscreet black,
Encircles the depressions of your eyes.
Not lifting your head,
In silent meditation, you watch
The black ribbons of your shoes
Weave in a triple coil.
Can one really take as lies
Your off-hand confessions
That you live eight lives,

Preserving memories of them all?...

We shall hope that the rather colorless quality of Leonid Berman's poems arises only from a noble uncertainty in his powers, and the desire, at any price, in every case, to gain a victory over theme.

Mikhail Dolinov has a preconceived idea—to write like the French poets of the eighteenth century and their Russian imitators. It is always suspect when a poet wants to be not himself but someone else. One is forced to think that he has no cherished ideas of his own, no expressions born for the first time. At best, skillful needlework results instead of poetry, but usually the Muse, present at the creation of every rhythmic speech, takes vengeance on those who have scorned her in some especially offensive way. And that is how it turned out in this case. Mikhail Dolinov is undoubtedly cultured and knows how to write verse, but he is a kind of Epikhodov in poetry, and failure—she is just as inspired as her sister success—torments him at every step, making him commit a series of blunders:

> Mountain spring of blessed indolence!
> I bent my shaggy knee...

...and only then does it become clear that the subject is not a man but a faun.

> I am bewitched by fables,
> I dream by the will of Phoebus:[3]
> That roses became birds
> And flew off to the heavens fast!

...in this stanza, which is not at all bad, the word "fast" produces a sharply comic effect and, alas, one not foreseen by the poet.

> Alas, I do not remember the date in May,
> And lie around all day like a blockhead...
> ....
> Your white marble is twined round with roses,
> And with a chain four posts stand joined...[4]

I was not being selective at all, and in almost every line there is something similar. And the really successful stanzas, which show that it is impossible not to call Dolinov a poet, drown in this sea of blunders:

> ...Or in the damp shadow of the copse,
> With his beloved girl, just the two,
> He reads acknowledged poets,
> Looking at himself in the reservoir...

Alexander Korona's book produces first of all an impression of great brazenness. It is called *Book of Songs.* In the first two poems, Pushkin's famous rhyme *"zarema-garema"*[6] is repeated five times. In the songs of Sulamith, reworkings of *The Song of Songs* are mixed with his own poems. Almost all the rest is too obviously inspired by Pierre Louys[7] and Kuzmin's *Alexandrian Songs.*[8] The epithets are accidental and careless, there is not even a trace of love for the sound quality of the word, and still, where the poet goes beyond his artificial themes of free love and daring sailors, he reveals, if not individuality, then at least talent.

Narcissus

> Why, tender youth,
> Do you rush to the banks of the river,
> Where the cold wind, at midday
> Flies into the reeds?
> Why, tender youth,
> Yielding to solitude, do you hurry,
> Steadfastly to solitude
> Do you fly with the light bird?
> Why, bending in solitude
> Over the limpid water, do you wait for someone?
> Tender youth, into the incomprehensible,
> You sing and do not sing.

This poem shows that Alexander Korona has "melodic power," but it appears only when he does not force it to serve other people's images and ideas.

In Chrolli's poems[9] there is both an easily accessible melodiousness and effectiveness, but approximate epithets and conventionally beautiful images. They undoubtedly satisfy the average

153

requirements for writing poetry now. However, it does not follow
that many write like this. Some, at the price of frequent failures,
strive for greater originality and significance, others, unable to attain even this level, carry new movements to an extreme to somehow camouflage their impotence. Chrolli's poems are not at all
bad, they are only hopelessly uninteresting, like something heard
a long time ago, and not from Bryusov or Blok, but from their
chance imitators. A poet like Chrolli must wait for some violent
shock, some great joy or sorrow, some highly significant meeting,
for his sluggish tongue to learn its words and for his fettered soul
to create a really valuable world for itself. And until that time, his
lot is crudely correct rehashings, as for example:

The Ship Sailing in

> The rapture of discovery and attack intoxicated her,
> The gales, the battles, the troubles in an unknown land,
> And a foreign genius called her to peace on the sea,
> And she boldly made foam of the submissive water.
> Oh, what mortal combat, what groaning, grating,
> She has survived the crack of masts and sails in the deep,
> Last prayers, stifled crackling
> And the fierce pressure of indomitable powers!

Anatoly Puchkov is an excellent example of a non-poet. He
has absolutely nothing to say, and he becomes tangled in words
and rhythms as if in some strong snares. It is difficult to make out
where metaphor ends and misunderstanding begins in his poems.
The rarest, most sonorous rhymes turn dull in them, for example
"*rozi-gryozi*." One often finds Futurist words in the book, and
one of the sections is designated the second notebook of "the Russian Symbolists." But we are not going to guess what he is, Futurist or Symbolist. His poems are outside these designations, because,
first of all, they do not belong to poetry.

Tikhon Churilin's poems[10] stand on the boundary between poetry
and something else very significant and enticing. Since ancient
times it has been held that prophets include their revelations in
poems, moralists—their laws, philosophers—their conclusions. It is

a characteristic fact that almost all madmen begin to write poetry. Any valuable or simply original attitude strives to be expressed in poetry. It would take too long to explain the reasons for this in this short note. But, of course, in most cases, this striving bears no relation to poetry.

Tikhon Churilin is a happy exception. In terms of literature, he is tied to Andrei Bely, and more remotely, with the Cubo-Futurists. He often manages to turn poems around so that ordinary, even well-worn words acquire a certain primordial wildness and novelty. His theme is the man approaching madness in real earnest, sometimes even the madman. But while real madmen describe little birds and flowers incoherently, there is in his poems the severe logic of insanity and truly delirious images.

> They shaved Kikapa—for the last time.
> They bathed Kikapa—for the last time.
>> With bloody water the basin
>> And his hair
>>> Where to, ma'am?
> Then you're his sister?
> Stay with him until morning if you like. . .

The theme of suicide as a means of escaping from the inexpressible suffering of life also attracts the poet. He is indebted to it for the best poem in the book.

End of the Clerk

> My pen, write, write,
> Scrape, scrape in the muffled silence.
> You, fall wind, dry
> The salt of my tears—blow, blow.
> My pen, write, write
> You, heart, brace all your force.
> Brace, brace. Scrape, scrape,
> My pen, buy me that thing.
> My happy hour will come—
> Go up, hopeless mole,
> And the gold piece—oh, I'm a terrible spender—
> I'll give it—and the salesman will take it.
> And I'll take that thing, take it,
> Clutch it to my heart.

155

> So quietly, quietly I'll clutch the trigger,
> And find peace and darkness.

One would like to believe that Tikhon Churilin will remain in literature and apply his keen sense of the word as material to less narrow and specialized themes.

Prince G. Gagarin[11] is a sort of improved Ratgauz. Is it possible that, side by side with the other traditions, there exists a tradition of lack of talent, lack of mental and poetic strength? And is it possible that this tradition continues to pose as some sort of celebrated "old school"?

In Prince Gagarin's work the verse is more melodious, the themes more varied than those of his prototype, but similarly, the main parts of every sentence consist of metaphors absolutely devoid of content. There is no internal link between words; they adhere only because they are printed one after the other. It is possible to remember them only if you cover your ears with your hands and cram, cram, as high-school students used to do. And it is well known that easy memorability of poems is one of the most unquestionable signs of their merit.

> My thoughts are a restless sea;
> With the borders of life in unceasing strife
> The surf beats and groans.
> Naked crags, barren cliffs,
> You raise in me an echo of harmony,
> Echo of the deep sea.

I included this poem in its entirety so that people would not criticize me for unfounded statements.

Count Alexander Saltykov[12] is probably very pleasant company. He has read a great deal, travelled, and is unquestionably educated. At worst we would expect from him a book of travel notes, a paper on ancient Italian religion, or finally, even a short story, nice in its old-fashioned sentimentality. But he should not write poetry at all. He gets helplessly muddled in meter and rhyme, his expressions are awkward, and his thoughts weak within the steel armor of the sonnet, his favorite form. He cannot manage without cliches, and his cliches are the most worn, the most dismal ones.

156

> ... On the shore, scarcely a sound ... deserted; solitary,
> Quiet is the expanse of sea ... The mists float there,
> Both the sea and the land are deep in thought;
> The bright Riviera gave itself up to quiet dreams.

It would seem difficult to attain a greater measure of disharmony of speech and inexpressiveness of image.

The most interesting section in the book, "Holy Year," is written in the form of a greatly simplified garland of sonnets, devoted to the description of the religious significance of the twelve months. But for some reason, the author has them introduce themselves, which is always somewhat comic. What is more, they are introduced in some sort of preposterous hodge-podge of Russian and Latin:

> I am Juno Sospita, I am Juno Populona ...
> Iuturna of Janus and also Dea bona.
> I, Mars' Neroi, I, Fauna of early days ...

No commentary will make such verses seem like poetry. Count Alexander Saltykov's book is a misunderstanding, arising from the fact that so few of us understand the essence and limits of poetry.

If we remember Andreev's story "In the Fog,"[14] a great deal will be cleared up in Vladimir Prussak's poems.[15] Otherwise, it is incomprehensible why he puts on such airs, first posing as a snob with bad manners à la Igor Severyanin, then a musical-comedy revolutionary proclaiming that art is higher than life and filling his poems with the names of his favorite authors. Why doesn't he write about what he has thought out instead of what he has thought up, if he wants to be a poet and not a filibuster in poetry —but is that perhaps what he really wants? Apart from the nervous debility, the thinness and weakness of spirit, the inability to choose and fight for what he has chosen, qualities he has in common with Andreev's hero, Vladimir Prussak seems to have an idea, very wide-spread among young poets, and extremely pernicious for them—the desire to be unlike other people, more petty and vulgar, perhaps, only not like other people. But, alas, only by following the common path of all men can one find one's individuality;

there is no stinking corner of thought where some cockroach-thinker is not already sitting, twitching his whiskers.

A dump?—there are as many dumps in literature as you please. The seduction of high-school girls?—and you will not find as many high-school girls as they have seduced in poetry and prose. Light-hearted strolls with prostitutes have been sung about hundreds of times. All this seems new only because it is easily forgotten. It is only some three or four years ago that Ego-Futurism appeared, and how old and dull it seems already. Vladimir Prussak must first dispel the cloud of clichés in his poems, before he can be spoken of as a poet.

Apollo, No. 10, 1915

XXXIV

Georgy Adamovich. *Clouds: Poems.* **Petrograd: Giperborei, 1916.**
Georgy Ivanov. *Heather: Second book of Poems.* **Petrograd: Altsiona, 1916.**
Mikhail Lozinsky. *Mountain Spring: Poems.* **Petrograd: Altsiona, 1916.**
Osip Mandelstam. *Stone: Poems.* **Petrograd: Giperborei, 1916.**

In his first book, *Clouds*, Geogry Adamovich[1] is an unestablished poet in many respects. He has neither enough technical experience nor enough skill to guess when a feeling has ripened enough for its realization. The book contains completely insignificant poems, and poems which are saved by a single brilliant image, a single successful stanza. However, throughout, we sense good training and proven taste, and sometimes glimpse an independence of thought which could grow into a special style or even a worldview.

I am speaking now of the gift of suitably adorning the coarse, gray cloth of everyday experiences and impressions with the golden threads of legend. Hearing the gramophone, where the police-officer seems to be grieving and the priest's wife's teeth aching, the poet remembers "how, hearing the night whistle, the Trojan vessels set sail with their marvelous spoils for the East." In an insipid, typically adolescent poem, without any development, telling how he is sailing somewhere, not on a river or on the sea, but, most likely, on life, the poet suddenly exclaims: "Or the magic boat will stop at the golden walls of Babylon."

But he does not love the cold splendor of epic images, he is searching for a lyric treatment of them and for that reason tries to see them illumined with suffering. To speak of the Sirens, he has to pity them, as voiceless:

> In hundred-colored steep ships
> The clouds do not sail the heavens,
> And the shores are covered with sand,
> And the glass river has dried up.
>
> But in the silence the stars still shine blue,
> And the sunken garlands wither,
> And the humpbacked grayhaired old men
> Freeze in the ruined tent.
>
> And the sirens, voiceless, dream,
> That from out the tent in silks and pearls,
> With a captivating smile on her lips,
> Comes the Shamakhian queen.

This sound of a tinkling string is the best thing in Adamovich's poems, and the most independent.

I mentioned this last poem because from time to time in the book you find rehashings of lines from Akhmatova, and for one poem it was even necessary to take an epigraph from Innokenty Annensky's "Ballad,"[3] they coincided so much in their images.

Georgy Ivanov's new book falls into two sections: *Heather* proper, and poems from the book *Chamber.*[4] I will deal only with the first, since I have already spoken of *Chamber* in the pages of *Apollo.*

Heather has a unifying purpose—the desire to apprehend and portray the world as a changing series of visual images. And a striving toward beauty inevitably brings the poet to retrospection and the description of works of art. Reading him, we seem to find ourselves in an antique shop. Here is an old portrait of Vasily's great-great-grandfather, crude, immaturely flat work, fit only for reproduction in *Capital and Country-seat*[5] (just like the poem). A stuffed clown with a stuffed dog. A beaded tobacco pouch—and the author gives an exact description of it, as in a catalogue.

159

"Coffee-pot, sugar-bowl, saucer," and so forth—in short, a whole tea service, and the poet even enumerates in detail who drank from it and when. And finally, an album of old colored lithographs, which are so nice to look over, and certainly with a magnifying glass. One is unlike the next, one more unexpected than the next, and they all make us happy with their reminder of life and nature, fully captured in line and color. In these works, Georgy Ivanov shows himself both a skillful master of verse and a sharp observer. He is able to create a whole from petty details and to indicate his attitude towards verse by its movement:

> How fine and sad to remember
> Flanders' inhospitable people:
> Father and son have dinner—and mother
> Serves potatoes on a flat plate.
>
> Green water shines in the window,
> The bank is yellow with seine and boat.
> Though there is no sun, I feel
> Its gentle flush so clearly.
>
> Subdued spirit above a life of work,
> Tranquil and alluringly rugged—
> In a land where the air, smelling of pitch,
> And the fishermen do not part with their pipes.

Georgy Ivanov's poems captivate with their warm texture and with a reality that, although limited, is unquestionable at first glance.

However, there are not only poems, there is the poet. And so it is sad not to find in *Heather* his earlier sweet and simple little songs, slightly "imitation Verlaine," reading which you do not know if feeling is so easily fettered by rhythm or whether rhythm itself engenders feeling, while the rhymes ring just like the clapping of children's hands in time to a simple dance. Three love poems at the end of the book, very much in the manner of Kuzmin, scarcely improve the situation. Why is that? Why does the poet only see, but not feel, only describe but not speak of himself, alive and real? But he hears the rhythm as before, that creative will of verse. An example is the splendid and rare combination of iambs and choriambs in the following poem:

160

The fishermen returned from fishing,
And the boulders grew dim,
On the straw roof lay
The rosy-gray shine of the moon.

Pricked-up ears
Listen to the slow surf:
The sea laps rhythmically, hollowly,
Like the ancient striking of a clock.

And above troubled waves,
In the darkening air, pale —
Behind the restless branches,
The moon rises.

I would like to end this short essay with a question, so that the poet will answer it for me with his next book. This is not a prediction. I have no basis for judging whether Georgy Ivanov wants and is able to seriously consider whether it is for him to be, or not to be, a poet, that is, to be always moving forward.

Mountain Spring is a good name for Mikhail Lozinsky's book,[6] because it is just as homogeneous and comes up from the depths in just the same way, but tells nothing of those depths.... Mikhail Lozinsky intensely, passionately attempts to realize his very distinctive and secluded world, and his poems are only rough notes which help him in this work.

With this same fate they also await the reader, to whom it will seem important and necessary to examine them, like a frayed, hand-drawn map of a distant island, full of smudges and blots. Such expressions as "hoary shroud of the incinerated past," "light of unanswered portents," "to the inexplicable city of the component order," "ash of instant," "blade of flashing pain"—all of these are carelessly devised, conventional symbols for designating perhaps genuine experiences, and, above all, they are in need of translation.

This idea that one must speak of the enigmatic enigmatically, of the unknown in expressions unknown until now, links Mikhail Lozinsky with some of our poet-Symbolists: Maximilian Voloshin, Yury Baltrushaitis, Vladimir Gippius.

However, having deciphered Lozinsky's cryptograms, you see

that you have not spent time in vain. What he speaks about is significant and beautiful; and the feat which only he tried to accomplish is a lofty feat. He wanted to remember the "unrememberable word," and at times we really believe that it has already tormented his lips:

> Meadow and heavens were lost
> In the damp and whitened haze.
> I heard the women's voices
> Growing distantly weaker.
> To my senses everything was
> So inexpressibly familiar
> As if now I would understand
> What was before, somewhere at home...

or:

> Today all day I
> Heard the voice of invisible bees,
> Like a fiery canopy
> Of lace, stirred by the heat.
> . . . .
> There are many words and songs
> For hearts obedient to sun-beams.
> They hear news of the distant,
> The stillness of aerial meadows....

It is gradually becoming clear why Lozinsky, as a poet, is devoid of visual and aural memory. He strains his memory so persistently, recalling heavenly melodies and aerial meadows, that he has no time and no desire to listen attentively to earthly sounds, to look carefully at earthly things. For him, our life is a dungeon, and he does not even favor it with condemnation, but merely stares intently upward, and phantoms of blue sky and dazzling rays at times vaguely flash before his gaze, weary from the strain.

This leads him to a Romantic arrogance, and almost every one of his poems could pass for a monologue of Manfred, Lucifer, Cain[7] and other splendid masks of late Romanticism. He also cannot do without newer literary reminiscences, principally from Balmont, and "Song of the Ships" reminds one of "Dead Ships."[8]

For about ten years now, Osip Mandelstam had been known and appreciated in literary circles. But the recently published *Stone* is his only book, because the little brochure of the same name[9] sold out quickly and scarcely reflected the complex paths of its author's work.

It is important to note first of all the complete independence of Mandelstam's poems. You rarely meet such complete freedom from any sort of outside influences. Even if he comes across a theme which has already appeared in another poet (which rarely happens), he reworks it to the point where it is completely unrecognizable. His only sources of inspiration have been the Russian language, whose most complex turns of speech he has had to learn, not always successfully, and his own seeing, hearing, palpating, eternally sleepless thought.

This thought reminds me of the fingers of a typist, so rapidly does it fly over the most diverse images, the most fantastic sensations, extracting the fascinating tale of an unfolding spirit.

The first period of Mandelstam's writing, from approximately 1908 to 1912, goes under the emblem of Symbolism, insofar as that elusive word explains anything for us. The poet strives toward the periphery of consciousness, to prehistoric chaos, into the kingdom of metaphor, yet he does not harmonize it according to his own will as do those who believe in all the doctrines; rather he is only frightened by the incompatibility between it and himself. "Silentium," with its bewitching invocation of pre-existence—"remain foam, Aphrodite,/ And word, return to music"—is nothing but an audacious amplification of Verlaine's *L'Art poétique*. In the enigmatic he senses a genuine danger to his human "self" and fears this with an animalistic terror:

> What if, over a modish shop,
> Eternally twinkling,
> Into my heart like a long pin
> The star were to suddenly drop?

Even his metaphor "Oh, the pendulum of souls, strict,/ Is swinging silent, straight" acquires an almost zoological existence. However, he is not yet perspicacious, he lives in half-sleep, and he himself defines his condition so correctly with the exclamation:

Is it possible that I am real,
And will death actually come?

The crisis comes in this poem:

No, not the moon, a bright clock-face
Shines at me, and why am I at fault
For feeling the frail stars' milkiness?
And the arrogance of Batyushkov repels me:
What time is it, they asked him then—
And he answered, bemused: eternity.

From this moment the poet becomes an initiate of the literary trend known by the name of Acmeism. He beautifully puts to use the knowledge that not a single image has independent significance, and that it is necessary only in order to reveal the poet's soul as fully as possible. Now he speaks of his human thought, love, or hatred and precisely defines their objects. By force of circumstance, as a city dweller, he became a poet of the contemporary city, although he never wonders, like a visiting bumpkin, at the automobiles and streetcars, and, visiting the library, he does not sigh over how much people have written, but simply takes the necessary book.

An approaching funeral, an old man who looks like Verlaine, Petrograd in winter, the Admiralty, janitors in heavy fur coats— everything rivets his attention, engenders in him thoughts that are so diverse, and yet unified by a single attitude.

For him, everything is pure, everything is a pretext for a poem: a book he has read, whose contents he retells in his own way ("Domby and Son"), the cheap romanticism of a movie scenario ("The Cinematographer"), a Bach concerto, a newspaper article on Imyabozhtsy, country-house tennis, etc., etc.

Although all the same he is most frequently concerned with architecture, with the ponderous masses of Notre Dame and the Hagia Sophia, and this is the avid gaze of a disciple upon the work of a master, of a disciple who dares to exclaim: "From the malignant heaviness I will someday create something beautiful."

But man has the characteristic of reducing everything to a unity; in this way, for the most part, he arrives at God. Osip Mandelstam has arrived at an idol—in love with reality, but not forgetting

164

his trembling before eternity, he has been captivated by the idea of the Eternal City, Caesarean and papal Rome. There he carries his dreams, tired from eternal wanderings, and from there he hears the chorus of archangels proclaiming Glory to God in the highest and on earth peace, good will toward men:

> ... And the dove does not fear thunder
> Which is the church's voice:
> In apostolic chorus: Roma!
> It alone makes the heart rejoice.
>
> I repeat the name
> Beneath the heavens' eternal dome,
> Though he who spoke to me of Rome
> He disappeared in holy dusk!

However, Rome is just a stage in Mandelstam's work, just the first symbol that came to mind of the power and magnificence of the creative spirit. The poet is already finding less common and more effective images for expressing the same feeling:

> ... Theater of Racine! A mighty veil
> Divides us from the other world;
> With its deep wrinkles undulating,
> A curtain hangs between it and us:
> Classicism's shawl falls from its shoulders;
> Fused by suffering, its voice grows stronger,
> seared with indignation, its style
> Achieves a sorrowful tempering...
>
> I came too late to celebrate Racine!
> . . . .

All this is related to questions of artistic vision. Problems of artistic creation are outlined in the profound and beautiful poems "The grain is poisoned, the air drunk up," and "I never heard the tales of Ossian," not to mention the earlier "Why is my soul so melodic."

I have pointed out only a few tendencies in the work of Osip Mandelstam, but I think even this is sufficient to show what a significant and interesting poet we are dealing with. In *Stone*, there are shortcomings, weak and confused poems, ear-splitting mistakes in language, but one does not wish to think or speak of this when reading a book of such rare value.

Apollo, No. 1, 1916.

XXXV

Mikhail Struve. *Flock: Poems.* **Petrograd: Giperborei, 1916.**

Here are poems of real mastery. Reading them, you forget that Mikhail Struve[1] is a young poet and that *Flock* is his first book. The decisive style of speaking, precise images and well-balanced composition make you accept his poems without reservation. One can sense his lack of great poetic experience only through indirect signs. In the first place, almost all the poems are written in iambs. Of course the iamb is simple, mobile, sonorous, and with its help the poet can cut thought nicely, like a diamond on a wheel. But the fact that all the themes and gusts of feeling fit easily into the iamb proves their uniformity. The poet has not yet heard the trochaic violins, the dactyllic gong, the anapestic bell and the rhythm of the sacred dances inherent in the amphibrach; he has no words it is necessary to stress in intervallic meters.

And what is more, most of the poems begin with a description of nature, a reference to some object. The lyrical emotion is too weak to burst out spontaneously, it is searching for a cause, almost an excuse. Besides that, too few themes are touched upon in this book. The clearly circumscribed impressions from the landscapes are somewhat meager, perhaps precisely because of this clarity and indisputability. The theme of a diseased conscience, one of the most curious traditions in Russian literature, going from Nekrasov and Dostoevsky to Leonid Andreev, is more interesting, but Mikhail Struve for the present has not found his solution to the questions it raises.

All of the above can serve neither as a reproach nor as a warning. Every poet develops according to laws he himself created, or rather, that arose with him, and here, haste is simply harmful. Let us remember that deep rivers always have a slow current.

The Stock-Exchange Gazette (morning edition), 30 September 1916.

Konstantin Lyandau. *At the Dark Door: Poems.* Moscow: Pashu-kanisa, 1916.

This book is the book of a man refined in the culture of verse, who has become introspective, reflective, melancholy, dreamy, but scarcely a poet.[1] For the poet is always the master of life, creating from it, as from precious material, his own image and likeness. If it turns out to be horrifying, agonizing or sad, it means he wanted it that way. The poet rejoices even in the riddles of life, just as a rider does in the horse's sudden leaps.

For Lyandau, everything is incomprehensible or unclear: there are more question marks in his book than in any other. What can he tell the world, he who even asks why "the fatigue of complete sin is trying?" For this is the limit of an inability to understand creatively. "To walk like a lifeless phantom" is scarcely the occupation of a poet, —if Pushkin, Hugo and Byron are poets. "I am afraid to say what I want"—this admission is so annoying that it even ceases to be moving.

There are naive critics who suppose that this is a special kind of poetry, pensive, tender, fragile. They should not be too lazy to go through all the collections of verse for the last hundred years in any language. A good half of them are written in precisely the same way, and no one has the strength to remember the names of their authors. What is so easily and completely forgotten possesses the gift of always appearing new. Konstantin Lyandau has still rendered a great service: in two lines he has explained to us the psychology of such work:

> In the nighttime silence, the scratching of the pen
> On the somnolent whiteness is tempting...

We can listen to the ringing of Apollo's lyre or the trills of Pan's flute—what good is the humble scratch of a pen?

The Stock-Exchange Gazette (morning edition), 30 September 1916.

XXXVII

Two Obituaries: Konstantin Mikhailovich Fofanov and Victor Victorovich Gofman.[1]

1. Konstantin Mikhailovich Fofanov is dead. With him Russian poetry has lost the last prominent representative of that movement which is characterized by the names of Golenishchev-Kutuzov, Apukhtin, Nadson, Frug and others. In the era of calm in the Eighties and Nineties he spoke of a world of good, of Spring, May, nightingales and lilies of the valley, and he made himself listen. His images, placid, unobtrusive, were quietly beautiful, although they resembled the kind of landscapes that were painted in those years. But sometimes he burned with a strength of expression and depth of thought. Such are his poems: "To the Decadents," "The Monster," and "The North Pole."[2]

2. He was a true poet, but one of those modest poets Longfellow dreamed on in his celebrated poem on the eve of renouncing "the grandiose poets, the bearers of great names, whose moans still echo in the hollow corridors of time."[3]

1. In Paris Victor Victorovich Gofman shot himself. The deceased wrote many stories and articles, translated much from German, but still the two books of poetry that remained are his most valuable literary legacy: *A Book of Preludes* and *Trial*. The first was especially successful in literary circles. A thing almost unprecedented—it immediately put the poet in the forefront and forced one to reckon with him, as with an unquestionably eminent figure. A free and singing verse, a passionate admiration for the beauty of life and dream, boldness of devices and a luxuriant variety of images, first outlined by him and subsequently turned into poetry— these are the distinctive traits of this book.

In the second book these qualities give way to a more weighty and resilient verse, to greater concentration and clarity of thought.

With these two books, despite an early death, Victor Victorovich Gofman insured himself a place among the poets of the second stage of Russian Modernism.

Apollo, No. 7, 1911.

XXXVIII

(Count Alexei Konstantinovich Tolstoi)[1]

-1-

Alexei Tolstoi himself described his life in a letter to the Italian professor, de Bubernatis, which we include below. It is necessary for us only to add a few details.

Alexei Tolstoi's parents were Count Konstantin Petrovich Tolstoi and Anna Alexeevna Perovskaya, the natural daughter of that well-known personage, Alexei Kirillovich Razumovsky. Their marriage was unhappy, and a few weeks after the birth of the child, the couple was separated forever.

The poet was broadshouldered, somewhat heavy, and was distinguished by his iron constitution and great physical strength: he bent copper five-kopek pieces in his hands and braided forkprongs like a woman's plait. In his youth, his features recalled Lev Tolstoi, to whom he was only very distantly related. He had a gentle character that yielded easily to female influence, first the influence of his mother, clever and power-seeking, then of his wife Sophia Andreevna Miller, Née Bakhmeteva, one of the most educated women of her time. A love of philosophy and comprehension of the secrets of existence were distinctively interwoven in him with a good-natured but pointed and refined humor.

He lived about half of his life abroad, for the most part in Germany, which, like many Russians of the middle of the last century, he was ready to consider his second homeland.

He died on the 28th of September, 1875, as a result of poisoning from the morphine to which he was forced to resort because of asthma.

-2-

In the forties, when Alexei Tolstoi embarked on his literary career, the heroic period of Russian poetry, characterized by the names of Pushkin and Lermontov, had ended. The new generation of poets, Tolstoi, Maikov, Polonsky, Fet, possessed neither the genius of their predecessors nor the wide range of their poetic interests. Contemporary Western poetry did not exert any appreciable

169

influence on them; the lucidity of Pushkin's verse became facileness in them, Lermontov's fever of soul—simple warmth of feeling.

Alexei Tolstoi's work is notable for its heightened *joie de vivre*. In his lyrics we see not only experiences, but their framework, the circumstances which engendered them; his historical ballads contain not only a description of events but an evaluation of them, often original, elucidating their significance for us. A staunch champion of freedom, an expert on European culture, Tolstoi loves to recall the Kievan period of Russian history, the civic spirit and intrinsic independence of the Kievan Rus, its constant and lasting tie with the West. The Moscow period arouses his horror and indignation, and its echo in the present—a pointed and bold ridicule. Because of this it was forbidden to stage his plays or to publish his poems. But this did not bring him the sympathy of the progressive youth on whose good opinion the poet sincerely prided himself, although he could not and did not wish to assume their taste. On the contrary, in a series of poems, he fought the then-prevailing materialist attitude toward life, proclaiming himself a devotee of pure beauty and a supporter of art, which did not please the progressive criticism of the time, and provoked not a few attacks on its part. He himself very correctly defines his position between the two poles of Russian social thought:

> Not a warrior of two camps, but only a chance guest,
> I would be happy to raise my good sword for the truth,
> But dispute with both was until now my secret lot,
> And not one could draw me to a vow;
> There will not be full union among us—
> Unbought by anyone, beneath whatever banner I stand,
> Unable to endure the biased zeal of friends,
> I would try to vindicate the honor of the enemy's banner.

-3-

Alexei Tolstoi first appeared in print in 1841 with the story "Vampire," published under the pseudonym Krasnogorsky. At that same time he began working on a long novel about the epoch of Ivan the Terrible, *Prince Silver,* which was fated to appear in print only in the sixties. From 1854 on, the poet published continuously. In the course of ten years, almost all his lyrics and the greater part of his long poems appeared. To this period belong his jokes and parodies under the pseudonym of Kozma Prutkov, written jointly with his cousins, Alexei and Vladimir Zhemchuzhnikov.[2] Then follows the work of many years on the dramatic trilogy *The Death of Ivan the Terrible* (1866), *Tsar Fyodor Ivanovich* (1868), and *Tsar Boris* (1870), interrupted by the writing of historical ballads. A drama on life in Novgorod, *The Governor*, was not finished, because the poet's wife disapproved of the beginning. It appeared only after his death.

The novel *Prince Silver* enjoyed the greatest circulation, printed in dozens of editions, and translated into all European languages. His poems and trilogy were also republished many times.

Printed as the foreword to the first volume of A.K. Tolstoi's Se-
lected Works (Berlin-Petrograd-Moscow: Grezhbin, 1923),
ed. Nikolai Gumilev. Only the first volume was completed.

XXXIX

(On Nekrasov)

(Gumilev's answers to a questionnaire sent out by Kornei Chukov-
sky[1] in 1921 to the prominent poets of the time, from Merezh-
kovsky to Mayakovsky—on their attitude towards Nekrasov and
his poetry.)

1. Do you like Nekrasov's poems?
   Yes. Very much.

2. Which of Nekrasov's poems do you consider the best?
   The epic-monumental type: "Uncle Vlas," "The Widower Admiral," "General Fyodor Karlych von Shtube," the description of the Tarbagatai[2] in "Grandpa," "Princess Trubetskaya," and others.

3. How do you regard Nekrasov's verse technique?
   Remarkably deep breath, power over the chosen image, remarkable phonetics, continuing Derzhavin over Pushkin's head.

4. Was there a period in your life when his poetry was more precious to you than the poetry of Pushkin and Lermontov?
> Youth: from 14 to 16.

5. How did you regard Nekrasov in childhood?
> I almost did not know him, and what I knew, I despised because of the estheticism.

6. How did you regard Nekrasov in your youth?
> Nekrasov awakened in me the idea of the possibility of the individual's active relation to society.

7. Does Nekrasov's influence show in your work?
> Unfortunately, no.

8. How do you regard Turgenev's famous assertion that in Nekrasov's verse "poetry didn't even stay the night"?
> A prosaist is no judge of a poet.

Printed in **Annals of the House of the Literati**, *No. 3, 1 December 1921. Akhmatova, Blok, Gippius, Vyacheslav Ivanov, Kuzmin, Mayakovsky and Merezhkovsky also answered the questionnaire. It was later expanded, sent to a dozen more poets and printed in Chukovsky's* **Nekrasov: Articles and Materials** *(1926).*

XL

Leaders of the New School
Konstantin Balmont, Valery Bryusov, Fyodor Sologub

Russian poetry had a splendid past. Such poets and Pushkin, Baratynsky, Tyutchev, Lermontov, Nekrasov, allowed it to catch up with the poetry of other European peoples. But changing conditions of life, the growth of cities, the flowering of philology, the discoveries of Western poetry, all this remained alien to it for a very long time. Only around the beginning of the twentieth century does it flourish anew and, one would like to believe, for a long time.

If one does not speak of precursors, three names characterize the beginnings of this dawn [*sic*].*

Konstantin Balmont proved to be foremost among them. He
traveled a great deal, translated a great deal. The collected works
of Shelley, Calderón, *Shakuntala, Snow-Leopard Skin*[1] (the Georgian national epos), etc. —these are his gifts to Russian literature.

But his chief service lies not in these translations—it lies in his
poems. Many now dispute the merit of his poems. They find them
too beautiful, too inexact in expression, too meager and affected in
thought. This may be true, but he did not write that way twelve
years ago. His three books of that period, *Burning Buildings,*
(1900), *Let Us Be Like the Sun* (1903) and *Only Love* (1903) will
remain forever in the memory of everyone who has read them, despite the fact that even they contain weak poems.

Konstantin Balmont was first to guess the truth, plain as day,
old as time, but very difficult to understand, that in the end,
poetry consists of words, just as painting consists of colors, music
of an alternation of sounds. He also guessed that words pronounced for the first time live, pronounced for the second time
exist and finally, pronounced for the third time, only are.

He burst violently into the peacefully grazing flock of old
words, all those "fallings in love, hopes, faiths, maidens, youths
and dawn," with new words: "devils, hunchbacks, cruelties, per-
versions" —everything that he himself picturesquely called "scimi-
tar words." True, behind them one can hear only the rustling of
paper, and not the distant rumble of life, but his rhythms are so
fascinating, his expressions so unexpected that one instinctively
wants to begin a study of the new Russian poetry with him. And
it is so pleasant to suddenly meet a woman of whom it is said:

> She has sea-colored eyes,
> She has a faithless soul

or a hunchback:

---

*A spelling mistake in the Russian. Gumilev uses the Russian word for dawn
"rassvet" instead of the word for "flourishing" or "flowering"—*"rastsvet."*

173

Look—the hunchback
Has such a mocking face,
That strange spine,
Satanic ring.

. . . .

And he instinctively smothers a laugh
And rejoices like a snake,
Because secret sin is
A distortion of being—

and many others, but most of all, the poet himself, as he appears
in one of his best poems:

Why is it so stifling, why is it so dull?
I've completely cooled toward dreams,
My days are uniform, my life monotonous,
I stand on the last line.
Only an instant is left, only a fleet-winged instant,
And I'll go off from pallid people,
Why do I linger before the open grave,
Not hurry into obscurity sooner?
I am not the ancient merry demigod, inspired,
I am not the genius of melodious dream,
I am the sullen hostage, the miserable captive,
I stand at the last line.
Only an instant is left, and the soul, like an albatross,
Flies off into the unknown gloom.
I am tired of moving from question to question,
I am sorry that I lived on earth.

. . . .

*An unfinished article begun in Paris in 1917, or in London in 1918.
The passage was first published in an article by G. P. Struve,
"From the Archives of Nikolai Gumilev: Unpublished materials for a biography of Gumilev and the history of literary
trends," in* **Tests** *(New York), No. 1, 1955, pp. 181-190.*

A NOTE ON SOURCES

All of the essays and reviews in this volume are translated from Nikolai Gumilev, *Sobranie sochinenii v chetyrekh tomakh,* ed. G. P. Struve i B. A. Fillipov, Washington, D.C. "Kamkin," 1968. Volume 4.

FOOTNOTES

THE LIFE OF VERSE

1. (c. 675-749). Gumilev may be alluding to his defense of ikon-worship or his revision of the Greek Orthodox Church's hymnbook.

2. François Coppée (1842-1908), French poet and playwright, known as the *poète des humbles*, contributor to the *Parnasse contemporain* (1866).

Sully-Prudhomme (1839-1907), French poet, Nobel Prize winner in 1901. In his later career his poetry favors the themes of the Parnassians.

Nikolai Nekrasov (1821-78), Major poet and influential editor, known primarily for his civic verse and advocacy of reformist and radical causes.

3. *Hérodiade* (1869), a dramatic poem, in which the heroine symbolizes the cold, sterile solitude of the esthetic life.

4. "The Critic as Artist; with some remarks upon the importance of discussing everything: a dialogue." *Intentions* (1891).

5. Semyon Nadson (1862-87), popular poet, also inspired by civic themes, whose verse, according to D.S. Mirsky, "marks the low-water mark of Russian poetic technique."

6. Charles Asselineau (1820-74), critic and novelist known for elegant and erudite reviews, and his *L'Histoire du Sonnet.*

7. Pierre de Ronsard (1524?-85), best known for his *Sonnets pour Hélène* (1578).

8. Turgenev's "A Quiet Backwater" is a short story (1854) in which the reading of Pushkin's poem "The Upas Tree" precipitates the suicide of Maria, who is hopelessly in love with a talented but frivolous man.

9. "The Poor Knight": a poem by Pushkin (1829); the knight has a vision of the Virgin Mary, takes a vow to fight for her, but in his fanatic devotion to the female image, fails to pray to God. Therefore the devils try, successfully, to take him to Hell. Aglaia Epanchin in *The Idiot* (Part II, Chap. 7) sees the knight as a man capable of blind faith in an ideal; she draws a parallel between the poem, Myshkin and Nastasya Fillipovna.

10. Sologub's "Night Dances: A Dramatic Tale in Three Acts," based on a fairy-tale from the famous Afanasiev collection. The role and power of the poet is a major theme. Fyodor Sologub (1863-1927) was a major Decadent, or Symbolist, poet and prose writer. Though best known abroad for his novels *The Petty Demon* and *The Created Legend*, connoisseurs of Russian poetry prize him for his elegant lyrics.

11. The Horae, goddesses of the Seasons in Greek mythology, are associated with many dieties, including Helios, but only as subordinate companions (whence Ivanov's "Heliads"). They number either three or four.

The Eridanus is a mythical river with the Electrides (Amber-) Islands at its mouth.

12. *Transparence* (Moscow: Skorpion, 1904) was Vyacheslav Ivanov's second book of poems. Gumilev reviews his *Cor Ardens* (part I in XIX, 1; part II in XXV) and *Delicate Secret* (XXIX), and discusses individual poems (XIII; XIX, 2; XXXII).

13. Kuzmin's *Chimes of Love (Moscow: "Skorpion,"* 1910), Mikhail Kuzmin's (1875-1936) musical pastorale in verse. Kuzmin was a composer, poet, dramatist, novelist, critic and translator; his essay "On Beautiful Clarity" (*Apollo*, 1910) is often seen as one of the first statements of Acmeist ideas. Translations into English include his homosexual novel *Wings: Prose and Poetry* (Ann Arbor, 1972) and the play *Venetian Madcaps* in *Russian Literature Triquarterly*, No. 7 (1973).

14. *The Scales* ceased publication in 1909, several months before "The Life of Verse" appeared in *Apollo*. Part IV of this article was apparently included by mistake. The poetry in *The Scales* is also discussed in XIII.

ACMEISM AND THE LEGACY OF SYMBOLISM

1. The reader should not think that with this phrase, I am burying all extreme trends in contemporary art. In one of the up-coming issues of *Apollo*, an article will be devoted to their examination and evaluation. [*author's note*]

2. Sedan, French city of great strategic importance on the Meuse River. Gumilev refers to the decisive battle of the Franco-Prussian War, fought there on 1 September 1870, which resulted in the surrender to the Prussians of 100,000 men under the command of Napoleon III.

3. Théophile Gautier (1811-72), French poet and novelist, forerunner of the Parnassian school.

THE READER

1. Paul Fort (1872-1960), French poet and dramatist. The poems of his forty volumes of *Ballades françaises* and *Chroniques de France* (1897-1951) are usually printed as prose paragraphs.

2. Théodore de Banville (1823-91), French poet and dramatist, member of the Parnassian school and contributor to the *Parnasse Contemporain* (1866).

3. The singer of psalms, that is, Solomon. The references are to the Song of Songs, v, e.g. 4:11, 5:13, 14.

4. Edward Bellamy (1850-98), American novelist and reformer, best known for his utopia, *Looking Backward: 2000-1887* (1888).

5. Gabriele D'Annunzio (1863-1938), Italian decadent writer, whose heroes are mainly concerned with developing a refined ability to experience sensual pleasure. The title character of his drama *La Gioconda* is a model for a brilliant sculptor who eventually deserts his wife for her, the true inspiration of his art.

6. Apparently, both this article and "The Anatomy of a Poem" were to be worked into a book on theory of verse that Gumilev planned during the last years of his life.

THE ANATOMY OF A POEM

1. Alexander Potebnia (1835-91), Russian philologist whose attempts to describe the nature of poetic creation in linguistic terms anticipated the linguistic or semiotic orientation of the Slavic formalist studies.

2. L'Avvaye. A group of French writers and artists, named for the house in Créteil they shared for 14 months (1906-07). Influential in spreading the ideas of Unanimism, introduced to them by Jules Romains, the group included Georges Duhamel, Pierre Jean Jouve and Charles Vildrac.

3. Dionysius the Areopagite, an Athenian mentioned in Acts xvii, 34 as converted by St. Paul's preaching in Rome. Works ascribed to him include 10 letters and a Liturgy.

4. Basil of Caesarea (Cappadocia) (c. A.D. 330-79), organizer of monastic communities in Asia Minor for which he composed ascetic rules, and later Bishop of Caesarea. His letters and sermons are among the best of the epistolography and rhetoric of his time.

5. Archpriest Avvakum (1621-82), a leader of the Old Believers, famous for his autobiography (1672-75).

ON TRANSLATIONS OF POETRY

1. Ermil Kostrov (c. 1755-96), poet and translator of Apuleius, Homer, Ossian, Voltaire and others. His translation of eight books of the *Iliad* was very popular even after publication of Gnedich's translation in 1829.

2. José Maria de Hérédia: see note 7, section XIV.

3. William Morris (1834-96), English artist, designer, poet and founder of the Kelmscott Press.

4. Jules Laforgue (1860-87), French poet associated with th Symbolists and an early experimenter with free verse.

5. This collection included articles by F.D. Batiushkov, Kornei Chukovsky and Gumilev. The text translated is from the second edition of the book (Petersburg, 1920).

177

I

· 1. Ancient Semitic goddess of fertility, beauty and love.

II

1. Stanislaw Przybyszewski (1868-1927), Polish poet and novelist. His novel *Homo Sapiens* was written in German (1895-98), and translated into Polish by the author (1901).

2. Sologub's poem "The Star Mair" ("Zvezda Mair," 1898).

III

1. Arion, Greek poet and musician (fl. c. 700 B.C.). According to legend, he was cast into the sea by mariners, but carried to Taenaros on the back of a dolphin.

IV

1. Evgeny Baratynsky (1800-44) and Nikolai Yazykov (1803-46) were, after Pushkin and Lermontov, the outstanding poets of the period.

Anton Delvig (1798-1831), one of Pushkin's closest friends, editor of the almanac *Northern Flowers* (1825-31).

Yakov Polonsky (1819-98), poet and translator, noted for his Romantic lyrics.

Apollon Maikov (1821-97), lyric poet who attempted to continue the Pushkin tradition, dealing with nature and Classical themes in refined poetic forms.

V

1. Herman Cohen (1842-1918), one of the founders of the Neo-Kantian Marburg school of philosophy.

Hiram, King of the rich and ancient city of Tyre, friend of David and Solomon (fl. 950 B.C.).

2. *Ashes.* SPb: Shipovnik, 1909. *Cup of Blizzards.* SPb., 1908.

3. Vladimir Benediktov (1807-73). Lev Mei (1822-62). Karolina Pavlova (1807-93).

4. The paeon is an antique four-syllable meter consisting of one long and three short syllables. The variations of the paeon are numbered as follows: (1) /- - - (2) - / - - (3) - - / - (4) - - - /. In tonic verse, the term is used to indicate a combination of two feet, in one of which an accent has been dropped.

VI

No notes in this section

178

1. Valerian Borodaevsky's collection was also reviewed in *Apollo*, No. 1, 1909 (VIII). He published one other collection in 1914.

1. Boris Sadovskoy (1881-1945), poet and short-story writer, began publishing in 1901. This was the first of several collections of poems, dealing mainly with stylized genre pictures of Russian life.

2. Ivan Rukavishnikov (1877-1930), minor poet, novelist, associated with the Symbolists. His novel *Accursed Race*, 1912, enjoyed considerable success. He published his works in 20 volumes (SPb., 1901-25). Gumilev refers to him again (XV) as a standard of bad taste.

IX

1. Vasily Zhukovský (1783-1852), lyric poet, voluminous translator and immediate poetic predecessor of Pushkin.

2. After the poem "Rolla" by Alfred de Musset (1810-57), which appeared in *La Revue des deux mondes*, 15 August 1833.

Peter Petrovich Potemkin (1886-1926), writer, playwright, critic and translator. A permanent contributor to the satirical magazine *Satiricon* after 1908, and later one of its editors. He emigrated in 1920.

4. Oblomov, lethargic hero of Ivan Goncharov's novel of that name, whose idyllic childhood was filled with food and frequent naps.

5. The references are to the heroines of Lermontov's *Demon* (1839) and Pushkin's narrative fragment *Cleopatra, or the Egyptian Nights* (begun 1825, resumed 1835).

6. *A Rebours (Against Nature,* 1884), a novel by the Decadent Joris Karl Huysmans (1848-1907) of des Esseintes' search for release from debilitating ennui in the exquisite and the perverse.

7. See above section V, n. 4.

8. Pavel Sergeevich Sukhotin (1884-1935), published three more collections of verse and several children's books.

9. Saint Petersburg shop owned by an assimilated French family. Originally Tait.

10. Sergei Krechetov (pseudonym of Sergei Alexeevich Sokolov, 1879-1936) emigrated after the Revolution, founded the "Medny Vsadnik" Press in Berlin, and published a literary almanac of that name.

11. Maurice Maeterlinck (1862-1949), Belgian-French poet, dramatist, essayist, Nobel laureate (1911).

12. Vladimir Lensky, the name of Pushkin's Schilleresque poetaster in *Eugene Onegin*, was the appropriately chosen pseudonym of Vladimir Yakovlevich Abramovich (1877-1926).

13. Alexander Stepanovich Roslavlev (1879-1920) is discussed disparagingly in XIV and XXIX.

14. Diary of Events.

X

1. *The Scales*, a monthly Symbolist literary journal published in Moscow (1904-09)

by "Skorpion" Press. Publisher, S.A. Polyakov (1874-1948). Editor, Valery Bryusov.

2. Ellis (pseudonym of Lev Lvovich Kobylinsky, 1879-1947), contributor to *Scales*, close friend of Andrei Bely and something of a Pushkinist. He emigrated to Switzerland before World War I.

3. *The Island*, a Petersburg almanac.

4. *Camelots*, Fr. "street-vendor."

XI

1. *Northern Flowers*, literary almanac (named after Delvig's St. Petersburg publication, 1825-32). Only five issues were published (1901-05) by the "Skorpion" Press, Moscow. Editor, Valery Bryusov. Initially including the works of Bunin, Chekhov, Rozanov, and unpublished writings of earlier writers—A.S. Pushkin, Tyutchev, Turgenev, Fet —it had become, by 1903, almost entirely a Symbolist publication.

2. Gumilev gave a much more favorable evaluation of Fofanov's work in the obituary that appeared in *Apollo* just over a year later (XXXVII).

3. Vasily Cholba and the other poets Gumilev mentions in this article apparently never published collections of their works again.

4. Iosif Simanovsky published his first collection of verse, *Zakatu*, in 1909 in an edition of 100 copies. It was printed, of course, in Bobruisk.

5. Bobruisk, rail junction in Belo-Russia, population 58,256 in 1890.

6. Toga praetexta, the official garment of the higher Roman magistrates, a toga bordered with purple. This title appeared on the dust jacket of the book by Rem and Sidorov.

7. Jacques Louis David (1748-1825), court painter to Bourbons and Bonapartes. Genrikh Ippolitovich Semiradsky (1843-1902), minor Russian painter.

XII

1. Gérard Walch (1865-1931). *Anthologie des poètes francais contemporains*: morceaux choisis, accompagnés de notices bio- et bibliographiques, et de nombreaux autographes. Paris: Delagrave, 1906. The immensely popular anthology gave its readers a survey of the poetic development of France in the second half of the XIX Century. The first three small 8VO volumes of approximately 550 pages each, contained works of over 250 poets.

2. Marie Catherine Le Jumel de Barneville, baronne d'Aulnoy (c. 1650-1705), author of stories and novels including *Les Contes de Fées* (1697) and *Nouveau Contes* (1698).

3. Anna Comnena Ducaena (1083-after 1148), daughter of Alexius I (reigned 1081-1118), wife of Nicophorus Bryennius, author of the *Alexiad*, the biography of her father from the start of his career through the struggle for the throne that followed his death, and the only Byzantine history written by a woman. The passage Gumilev mentions reads:

> For all my desire to name their leaders (the Crusaders), I perfer not to do so. The words fail me, partly through my inability to make the barbaric sounds—they are so unpronounceable—and partly because I recoil before their great numbers.
>   —pp. 324-25, Chapter X, *The Alexiad of Anna Comnena*, translated by E. R.A. Sewter, Penguin Books, 1969.

4. Daniil Maximovich Ratgauz (1869-1937) published collections of his mediocre

verse with ruthless regularity from 1900 until the Revolution. Later, he printed at least one collection in Berlin.

     5. *Poltava* (1828-29), Pesn' 2, 11. 268-69. *Polnoe Sobranie Sochinenii*, Vol. 5, p. 43.

XIII

     1. *World of Art*, luxuriously illustrated, beautifully designed bi-weekly, later monthly journal of the arts and letters published in St. Petersburg (1899-1904) by Sergei Diaghilev and Alexander Benois. Its literary contributors included Zinaida Gippius, Merezhkovsky, Minsky, Rozanov, Bely and Bryusov.

     2. Minsky (pseudonym of Nikolai Vilenkin, 1855-1937), an early proponent of esthetic evaluation in Russian criticism.

     3. *New Path*, literary journal published in St. Petersburg (1903-04), founded by three former members of the *World of Art* circle—Gippius, Merezhkovsky and D.V. Filosofov (Diaghilev's cousin, 1872-1942).

     4. Skorpion, Moscow publishing house (1900-1916) owned by Sergei Polyakov (1874-1948). It was the first house in Russia to publish the new Western literature, including Verlaine and Verhaeren, and the books of the Russian Symbolists Bely, Bryusov, Gippius, Sologub, Ivanov. Skorpion produced the literary almanac *Northern Flowers* (1901-05) and the journal *Scales* (1904-09). It paid great attention to the artistic aspect of its publications, employing artists from the *World of Art* group, including Somov, Bakst, Sudeikin.

     5. *Urbi et orbi: Poems 1900-1903.* Moscow: "Skorpion," 1903. *Garland (Stephanos): Poems 1903-1905.* Moscow: "Skorpion," 1906.

     6. Henri Farman (b. 1874), pioneer French aviator and inventor. In 1909 he set a world record for flight duration and altitude.

XIV

     1. Maenades, also Bacchae or Thyiades, women inspired to ecstatic frenzy by Dionysius.

     2. Andromache, in the *Iliad*, the daughter of Eetion, King of Thebes, and wife of Hector. She appears in Euripedes' *The Trojan Women* and is the heroine of his *Andromache*.

     3. Echafaudage, Fr. "scaffolding."

     4. Alexander Roslavlev's first book, *In the Tower*, was published SPb., 1907; after this review, he published only two "tales in verse" in 1915.

     5. Mikhail Artsybashev (1878-1927), novelist and playwright. The frank discussion of sex in his novel *Sanin* (1907) created a sensation.

     6. Evgeny Kurlov (1876-?) published only one other small collection of poems in 1915.

     7. José Maria de Hérédia (1842-1905), Cuban French poet best known for *Les Trophées* (1893) which includes 118 sonnets.

     8. Alexander Rotshtein. These *Sonnets* are his only collection.

     9. Marcel Schwob (1867-1905), essayist, poet, novelist. His last book and masterpiece, *Vies imaginaires* (1896) is a collection of re-created lives of nearly forgotten philosophers and writers.

     10. Vasily Knyazev (1887-1937 or 38) became an important satiric poet after the Revolution, and although he took part in the proletarian literary movement, was "repressed" in the late 1930s, and died at Kolyma. Posthumously rehabilitated, 1956.

11. Dmitry Minaev (1835-1889), poet, publicist and translator.

12. Otto Weininger (1880-1903).

13. Vasily Stepanovich Kurochkin (1831-1875), poet of revolutionary spirit, editor of *The Spark*.

Peter Veinberg (1831-1908), poet and translator of Heine, Schiller and Shakespeare.

XV

1. Nedotykomka, the dusty demon that harasses Peredonov in Sologub's novel, *The Petty Demon*, 1907.

The poem "The Star Mair."

2. Lord Ravenswood's son Edgar is the hero of Walter Scott's *The Bride of Lammermoor* (1819), which was the basis for Donizetti's opera *Lucia di Lammermoor* (1835).

3. Alexei Apukhtin (1840-93), lyric poet popular in the 1880s. Many of his lyrics were set to music by his old school friends Tchaikovsky and Moussorgsky. Gumilev mentions him disparagingly later in this essay and in XXXI.

4. Nikolai Morozov (1854-1946) spent twenty-five years in Schlusselberg Fortress for revolutionary activities (1881-1905), during which time he wrote twenty-six manuscript volumes on the natural sciences, and a number of poems, published (SPb., 1906) under the title *Out of the Walls of Bondage*.

5. René Ghil (1862-1925), Flemish French poet, systematized his conception of "scientific poetry," according to which each consonant and vowel possesses a particular timbre or musical value. His scientific concepts and musical technique are applied in his *Oeuvre* (1889-1909). He was in correspondence with Bryusov, and contributed to *Scales,* and later *Apollo* and *Russian Thought*.

6. Tatiana's letter to Onegin, 11. 22-23. (Chapter III, following Stanza XXI).

7. Nikolai Brandt published two more collections of poems (Kiev, 1912 and 1913) after this, his second book.

8. The anthropoid mandrake, said to scream when uprooted.

9. Sergei Gedroits (pseudonym of Vera Ignatevna Gedroits?). Despite the scathing review, *Flight*, a small collection of poems by S. Gedroits, appeared in 1913, published by Gumilev's Guild of Poets, and both appeared in *Almanac of the Muses* in 1916.

XVI

1. This posthumous collection of Yury Sidorov's poems was his first.

2. Vladimir Benediktov (1807-1873), minor poet and favorite of parodists.

3. Yaldabaoth. The meaning and origin of the word are unclear. In gnostic writings, it refers to the malevolent false god who created the material world. He was the offspring of rebellious Sophia (knowledge).

4. Iurii Verkhovsky (1878-1956), poet and translator of Bocaccio's *Ninfale fiesolano* and other works of Renaissance poets.

5. The reference is to Zhukovsky's philosophical poem "Theon and Aeschines," 1814.

6. Penates, guardian gods of the family, household gods. Alphea, a river in the Peloponnesus.

7. The second edition (1912) of Negin's "dramatic epic" was a larger printing.

XVII

1. Modest Druzhinin continued publishing until the Revolution. The three books referred to are all entitled *Poems*, 1909 and 1910.

2. Antonov's 36-page collection was published in 1910 in 120 copies. It is his only published work.

3. Vladimir Gessen (1868-1919): a famous lawyer's only book of poems.

4. Baron N.A. Vrangel. *Poems (Stikhotvoreniia*, 1911) is his sole published work.

5. Sergei Alyakrinsky published a second collection, *Cactuses (Kaktusy*, 1912).

6. Alexander Fedorov (1868-1949) prolific poet, prose writer and translator. Gumilev apparently refers to the second edition of his *Stikhotvoreniia* (1909).

7. Imatra, a picturesque waterfall frequented by Romantic poets, on the Wuoksi River, the largest and longest in Finland.

8. Dmitry Svyatopolk-Mirsky (1890-1939 or 1941), the famous literary historian and critic, published no more verse.

9. E. Astori's sole published work.

10. E.I. Shtein's book is entitled *I (Ia*, 1910).

11. Sofia Semenovna Dubnova (b. 1885) published a second book *Mother (Mat'*, 1918).

12. Emelyanov-Kokhanovsky (pseudonym of Alexander Nikolaevich Emelyanov, (?-1900). His book, *Bared Nerves (Obnazhennye nervy*), was published in three editions (1895, 1903, 1904). To the second and third were added a portrait, an autobiography and an "especially funny section" entitled "Tears of a Balding Devil."

13. Anastasia Verbitskaya (1861-1928), writer of tremendously popular novels for women, dealing with sex, free love, and contemporary problems in lengthy melodramatic plots.

14. Severyanin has made an adjectival form from the pejorative "mek" (Menshevik), and added a Russian ending to the French word "grisette."

15. Fyodor Kashintsev continued to write abroad after the Revolution.

16. F. Lado-Svetogorsky's book is entitled *Songs of the Bright Land (Pesni o svetloi strane,* 1911).

17. Sergei Klychkov (pseudonym of Sergei Antonovich Leshenkov, 1889-1940), continued writing both poems and novels. *Dubravna* was published in 1918.

18. Elisabeth Böhm (1843-1914), minor Russian painter. Her sentimental illustrations of Russian proverbs, with cherubic, pink-cheeked children in Russian costume, were popular around 1910.

19. Modest Lyudvigovich Gofman (1890-1959), had previously published a collection *Ring (Kol'tso*, 1907).

20. *Hatchery of Judges*, 1910 almanac in which the group of poets later called Futurist (Khlebnikov, Kamensky, the Burlyuks, Elena Guro) appeared for the first time. The title, Khlebnikov's invention, is ambiguous. As translated, it suggests that the book is a cradle containing the new judges of Russian criticism; but another translation is *Trap for Judges*, meaning that the critics are sure to misjudge it. Although Kamensky and Burlyuk insisted the book was a sensation and marked the dawn of a new era, only about 20 copies went on sale because the authors could not pay the printing bill. Gumilev discusses *Hatchery of Judges II* (1913) in XXX.

21. Alexei Mikhailovich Remizov (1877-1957), novelist and essayist.

22. Marsyas, a Phrygian peasant or satyr who picked up the flutes Athena had thrown away because they distorted her features. He was so successful that he challenged Apollo to a contest, which he lost. Marsyas was flayed alive for his presumption.

23. Maria Bashkirtseva (1860-84), diarist and painter, began *The Journal of a Young Artist*, for which she is famous, at age 12.

XVIII

1. Vladimir Kulchinsky's only collection of poetry is compared to Vasily Trediakovsky's verse translation of Fenelon's *Telemaque* (1766), famed for its tediousness and ineptitude.
2. Konstantin Bolshakov (1895-1940), minor Futurist poet.
3. Alexander Diesperov no longer published after this, his first book.
4. *Golden Fleece*, a heavily illustrated monthly art and literary journal (Moscow, 1906-09), in which Blok, Vyacheslav Ivanov and Georgy Chulkov took a leading role. For the first six months, it was published in Russian with the French *en regard*.
5. *The Pass,* anthologies published irregularly between 1924 and 1928 (six issues appeared), by the circle of writers of the same name.
6. "Grif"—an important publishing house.
7. Vladimir Narbut (1888-1938?), later one of Gumilev's fellow Acmeists, and a literary bureaucrat after the Revolution, he died in the purges.
8. Lev Zilov (1883-1937) published sixteen books of poetry for children (through 1929).
9. Boris Zaitsev (1881-1972), prose writer, dramatist, translator, biographer of Russian writers, his first story was published in 1901, his first collection in 1906. He emigrated in 1922, and lived most of his life in Paris, where his translation of the *Divine Comedy* was published (1961).

XIX

1. *Eugene Onegin*, "Fragments from Onegin's Journey," 9. 2-5.
2. Ghazal, also gazel, ghazel, ghasel, ghazul, a form of lyric poetry of Near Eastern and Central Asian peoples, composed entirely of couplets with a recurring rhyme: aa, ba, ca, da, etc., and limited to five, ten or fifteen stanzas.
3. Vitold Frantsevich Akhramovich (Ashmarin) (d. c. 1938).
4. *Poems (Stikhotvoreniia): Elegies, Odes and Idylls,* SPb, 1909, discussed in VII, VIII.
5. Maximilian Voloshin (-Kirienko) (1877-1932), poet, translator, painter, friend of all the major Symbolists.
6. Kimmeriitsy lived near the straits connecting the Sea of Azov to the Black Sea. There was an important Greek colony founded there by the Meletians which during the Persian Wars became an independent, half-Greek, half-barbarous state, later destroyed by the Scythians.
7. Samuel Kissin (1888-1916), prolific poet, short-story writer, dramatist, began publishing under the pseudonym "Muni."
8. *Songs (Pismi)*, Altsiona Press, Moscow, 1911; discussed in XVII.
9. Sergei Raevsky apparently never published a collection of poems.
10. Georgy Rachinsky (1853-1939), associated with religio-philosophical circles in Moscow.
11. Semen Rubanovich never published a collection of poems.
12. Sergei Ryumin apparently never published again.
13. Margarita Vladimirovna Sabashnikova (b. 1882), painter and poet, advocate of anthroposophy, wife of Maximilian Voloshin, she published her memoirs in Germany.
14. *Niva*, illustrated weekly (SPb., 1870-1918) with a wide circulation (275,000 by 1917). From 1894 to 1916, there were monthly literary supplements containing the complete collected works of Tolstoy, Turgenev, Leskov and other Russian writers.
15. Lyubov Stolitsa (1884-1934). Her best known work is her novel in verse *Elena Deeva,* published in four editions (1916-1923). She emigrated to Bulgaria.

1. Konstantin Somov (1869-1939), painter, book illustrater, contributor to *The World of Art*. He is famous for his covers of Symbolist publications including Balmont's *Firebird* (1907), Ivanov's *Cor Ardens* (1911), and the first edition of Blok's dramatic works (1907).

2. Jayadeva, Indian poet (XII Century, A.D.), probably Bengali, author of the lyrical dramatic epic *Gitagominda*, the story of the love of Krishna for the beautiful shepherd Radga.

3. *Letters of a Russian Traveler* (1790-91) by Nikolai Karamzin (1766-1826).

4. D. Navashin never again appeared in print.

1. Skorpion, cf. XIII n. 4.

2. *Poems*, Paris, 1910.

3. Terza rima, iambic tercets rhyming aba, bcb, etc.; invented by Dante.

4. Graal Arelsky (pseudonym of Stepan Petrov, 1889-?), one of the founders of Ego-Futurism.

5. *Burning Buildings: A Lyric of the Contemporary Soul* was first published in Moscow in 1900.

6. S. Konstantinov, despite the favorable review, never published another book.

7. This collection, printed in Rostov-na-Donu, is the only published work of S. Tartakover, who is rather better known as a chess-player.

8. Haim-Nakhman Byalik (1873-1934), Jewish poet, novelist, translator, publisher in Odessa, Berlin, Tel-Aviv, b. Kishinev.

Sholom-Ash (Sholem Asch, 1880-1957) was born in Poland and emigrated to the United States in 1910 to become one of the most prominent American Jewish novelists and playwrights. His first success was *God of Vengeance*, produced by Max Reinhardt in Berlin, 1910.

Some of the early works of both writers were in Yiddish.

9. This is Konge's only publication, and he seems to have vanished altogether. There is even some confusion about the spelling of his name (cf. Tarasenkov, *Russkie Poety XX veka: Bibliografiia*. Moscow: Sovetskii Pisatel', 1966. p. 450 "Kenge," p. 128 "Kengs").

10. Mikhail Dolinov published another collection, *Rainbow* (Raduga, 1915), discussed in XXXIII.

11. Lev Vasilevsky (1876-1936) began writing poetry in 1902. He later published only one short piece, in 1912.

12. Alexander E. Kotomkin emigrated after the Revolution and continued to write indifferent civic verse in Prague.

13. Yury Zubovsky (1890-?) never published another collection of verse.

1. *Song of the Merchant Kalashnikov* (1836), patriotic historical epic inspired by the reign of Ivan the Terrible, written by Mikhail Lermontov (1814-41).

2. Ilya Muromets and Alesha Popovich, together with Dobrynya Nikitich were the principal heroes of the Kievan cycle of epic songs (*byliny*). Dyuk Stepanovich, a bogatyr of foreign name and half-Russian origin, was in some accounts from India, Karelia or Volhynia.

3. Nikolai Klyuev published his first two collections in 1912: *Chime of the Pines* and *Fraternal Songs,* discussed in XXV.

4. Archistrategos, Greek, "chief commander," epithet for Michael, the angel of the sword and conqueror of Satan.

5. Luke, II, 14.

6. According to one tradition, Adam, fashioned of baked earth, was somewhat overdone.

7. Klysty (Flagellants), a mystical religious sect formed in the mid-seventeenth century, during the Schism.

8. François Villon (1431-?) author of *Le Grand Testament* (1461). His popularity in the late nineteenth century as a picaresque hero was based on colorful and for the most part legendary episodes in his life.

9. *Romances sans paroles* (1874) and parts of *Sagesse* (1880) are the most Rimbaudian of Verlaine's poems.

10. *Mèmoires d'un Veuf (Notes of a Widower*, 1886) is the only prose work Gumilev discusses in his "Letters on Russian Poetry."

11. Vadim Shershenevich (1893-1942), poet and translator, author of a dozen collections of poetry (between 1911 and 1926), Symbolist, Ego-Futurist, and eventually the main theorietician of the Imaginists.

XXIII

1. Cythera, island off the south coast of Laconia, where Aphrodite was said to have landed after her birth in the sea.

2. Mikhail Zenkevich (b. 1891), minor Acmeist poet, translator of Shakespeare, Whitman, Hugo, Freiligrath and Njegoš.

3. Commodus (Lucius Aelius Aurelius Commodus), 161-92, Roman emperor (180-92), son and successor of Marcus Aurelius. He vaunted his strength in the arena and decreed he would be worshipped as Hercules Romanus.

Ahura Mazda (also Ormazd), in Zoroastrian scripture, the triumphant leader of the forces of good in the war against evil.

XXIV

1. Cf. Gumilev's review in XVII.

2. Pavel Radimov (b. 1887). His second book, *Earthly Raiment* (1914), is reviewed in XXXII. He published two collections after the Revolution.

3. J.H. Rosny aîné (pseudonym of Joseph Henri Honoré Boëx, 1856-1940). French novelist, among the original members of the Goncourt Academy. Until 1909, he collaborated with his brother Seraphin Justin François Boëx (1859-1948).

4. Charles Marie René Leconte de Lisle (1818-1894). French poet, leader of the Parnassians. His collection *Poémes barbares* (1872) established his reputation.

5. Francis Jammes (1868-1938). French poet and novelist. His pastoral poems describe his native region of the Pyrenees.

6. Vsevolod Kurdyumov published five more collections of verse before the Revolution. With the exception of *Powdered Heart* (1913), which is reviewed in XXIX, they were printed in editions of 80 copies or fewer. In 1924 he published satirical propaganda pieces.

7. Anatoly Burnakin worked for the reactionary St. Petersburg daily *The New Time* (1868-1917) until the Revolution. This was his single collection of verse.

8. Sasha Cherny (pseudonym of A. M. Glikberg, 1880-1932) wrote satirical verse

and children's stories; worked with Mayakovsky on *The Satiricon* (1906-17, a magazine devoted to political and social satire). He emigrated to France in 1920.

XXV

1. Ivanov's *Cor Ardens* (*The Ardent Heart*. Moscow: "Skorpion," 1911) was published in two parts. Part I—*Cor Ardens: Speculum Speculorum* is reviewed in XIX. Part II—*Love and Death: Rosarium* (*Rose Garden*).

2. Maya, a term in Hindu Vedantic philosophy.

3. Perseus, hero of ancient Greece, slayer of the Gorgon Medusa, savior of Andromeda, founder of the Perseids.

4. Basileus, Persian Emperor, fifth century, B.C.

5. *Chime of the Pines* (1912) is discussed in XXII.

6. Cf. Luke X, 40-42.

7. The subtitle of Klyuev's *Fraternal Songs* is *Songs of the Golgothian Christians*.

8. Kunstkammer, literally "art chamber"; in Russian, a cabinet of curiosities.

9. The first edition of Narbut's *Hallelujah* (1912) was confiscated by the censors.

10. Count Peter Bobrinsky printed another collection *Pandora* (1915).

11. Feelings are normally carried "in the heart" in Russian; pregnant women carry children beneath the heart ("pod serdtsem").

Armor may be *zazubrennyi* (jagged, notched), but so can multiplication tables and lists of Latin verbs (learned by rote).

12. *The Sphinx*, first published June 11, 1894, but really dating from his Oxford days, was little more than an experiment with words. He delights in rhyming sarcophagus, catafalque and obelisk with Tregolephos, Amenalk and basilisk.

XXVI

1. Pierrot, Piero, Pedolino, a Commedia Dell' arte character dating from the second half of the seventeenth century. A charming and unusually trustworthy valet dressed in a white shirt with long sleeves, heavily powdered and maskless, he was often the rival of Harlequin for the love of an artful serving maid, usually Columbine.

2. Pushkin's *Gavriiliad*, April, 1828.

3. Dante's *La Vita Nuova* (c. 1293), a short work containing his early sonnets and canzoni with prose commentary.

Ronsard's *Sonnets pour Hélène* (1578), one of his last works.

Goethe's *Die Leiden des jungen Werthers* (1774).

Baudelaire's *Les Fleurs du Mal* (1857).

4. *Earth in Snow: Third Collection of Verse*. Moscow: Zolotoe Runo, 1908.

Night Hours: Fourth Collection of Verse. Moscow: Musaget, 1911.

These were combined in the third volume of the 1912-13 collection of Blok's verse under the title *Snowy Night*.

5. *Nets* (Moscow: "Skorpion," 1908) was Kuzmin's first collection.

6. Hafiz (Shams-ud-din Muhammed, c. 1300-89), Persian lyric poet whose collection, *The Divan of Hafiz*, includes more than 500 ghazals.

XXVII

1. Byliny, epic folk songs relating the deeds of the bogatyrs and set against the background of the court of Prince Vladimir Svyatoslavich of Kiev.

2. Vladimir Bestuzhev (pseudonym of Vladimir Vasilevich Gippius, 1876-1941) had earlier published a collection under the name of Vladimir Neledinsky (*Vspyshki*, 1905); literary critic and translator.

3. Poe's sonnet "Silence" (first published April, 1840 in *Burton's Gentleman's Magazine*).

XXVIII

1. Boris Abramovich Gurevich's book was confiscated by the censors. He had earlier published another collection *To My People*, 1913.

2. Alexander Ivanovich Tinyakov (Odinoky), 1886-1922, a contributor to various Modernist journals. Two collections of his verse were published after the Revolution.

3. Nikolai Nikolaevich Zhivotov published several other collections, all in the city of Ananiev.

XXIX

1. Vadim Danilovich Gardner (1880-?). This was Gardner's second collection. He emigrated to Finland after the Revolution.

2. Alexei Skaldin (1889-1943). This is his only collection of poems.

3. Sergei Solovyov (1885-1941), nephew of the poet and philosopher Vladimir Sergeevich, friend of Bely and Blok. This is the fourth of five collections published before the Revolution. His *April* (1910) is reviewed in XV.

4. Yakov Lyubyar (pseudonym of Alexei Lozino-Lozinsky, 1888-1916) published two more small collections of verse in 1916.

XXX

1. *Hatchery of Judges II* was published by the Hylaea group (cf. XXI n. 9), but as in the first *Hatchery of Judges*, the name did not appear because of Guro's objections. The collection appeared in February, 1913, and opens with a manifesto (as in *A Slap in the Face of Public Taste*).

2. Elena Guro (Notenberg, 1877-1913), Futurist poet, writer and painter; she signed only some of the early Futurist manifestos, contributed to their publications, but rarely participated in their public appearances.

3. Benedikt Konstantinovich Livshits (1887-1939), Futurist poet and translator. His first collection *The Flute of Marsyas* (1911) is reviewed in XVII. He also wrote a book of memoirs, *The One-and-a-Half-Eyed Archer* on the history of Futurism.

4. Velimir (Viktor Vladimirovich) Khlebnikov (1885-1922). His contributions to various publications are discussed in XVII and XXXI.

5. Nikolai Burlyuk (1890-1920), Futurist prose writer and poet, brother of David Burlyuk.

XXXI

1. It soon became an open secret that despite his repeated denials, Bryusov was the author of the *Nelli Poems*.

2. E.T.A. Hoffmann's tale "The Golden Bowl" ("Der Goldene Topf," 1814).

3. *Russian Thought*, scientific, political and literary journal, published monthly,

Moscow, 1880-1918. In the 1910s Bryusov handled the literary section, and Zinaida Gippius the critical material.

4. Volapuk, artificial international language based on Western European languages, created in 1879. Although there were many Volapuk societies in the 1880s publishing journals, textbooks and grammars, the language's popularity had sharply fallen by 1895.

5. Schematist (Russ. *Skhimnik*), a monk who has taken the vows of schema, the strictest monastic rule in the Orthodox Church.

6. Ambroise Thomas (1811-1896), French operatic composer. His triumph *Mignon* (1866), given over a thousand performances in less than thirty years, was based on Goethe's novel *Wilhelm Meisters Lehrjahre.*

7. The quotation is from Severyanin's brochure "Prologue of Ego-Futurism" (November, 1911), where he suggests that Pushkin is old-fashioned by comparing him with Gavrila Derzhavin (1743-1816), perhaps Russia's best eighteenth-century poet.

8. Kozma Prutkov, a joint pseudonym of A.K. Tolstoi and his cousins Alexei and Vladimir Zhemchuzhnikov for their satirical verse and parodies.

9. Hylaea, the Greek name of Scythian lands near the Black Sea, chosen by Benedikt Livshits and the Burlyuks as the name of the literary circle that was to become the Futurists. Khlebnikov, Kamensky, Guro, and soon Mayakovsky and Kruchenykh joined them. The group became known as the "Cubo-Futurists" in 1913, but "Hylaea" was not abandoned.

10. *Studio of the Impressionists* (published SPb., February, 1910, about two months before *Hatchery of Judges*) contains several poems by the Futurists David and Nikolai Burlyuk and Velimir Khlebnikov.

11. The words are all from one of Khlebnikov's best known poems "Incantation by Laughter," published in 1910 in *Studio of the Impressionists.*

12. "Private viewing," Russ. *vernisazh*, from the French *vernissage*—varnishing, varnishing day, the opening day of an art exhibition.

13. Aquilò—L. the North wind, the wind.

14. Count Vasily Komarovsky (1881-1914), began publishing only in 1912, with five poems and a short story in *Apollo*. Gumilev discusses his only collection. The rest of his works, short stories, lyrics, a narrative poem and a novel, remained unpublished. Count Komarovsky suffered periodic attacks of madness.

15. Henri de Régnier (1864-1936), French poet, novelist and critic. Under the influence of Jose Maria de Hérédia, his later works combined classical form with occult themes and the sumptuous decorativeness retained from his early association with Mallarmé.

16. Constantinople, like Rome, was built on seven hills.

Riza, metal covering of an ikon which allows only the face and hands of the image to show.

17. Johann Gottlieb Fichte (1762-1814). German philosopher, later remembered more as a patriot and liberal.

18. "Le Voyage" was one of the three poems added to the second edition of *Les Fleurs du Mal* in 1861. It is the last poem of the book.

19. Three plays on classical themes:

King Ixion: Tragedy in five acts with musical interludes. SPb.: M.P. Frolovoi, 1902.

Melanippe the Philosopher: Tragedy. SPb.: M.P. Frolovoi, 1901.

Laodamia: Lyric tragedy in four acts with musical interludes. SPb.: 1902.

20. Annensky's play is loosely based on a myth concerning Philammon, poet and musician of the pre-Homeric period, said to be the son of Apollo, and closely associated with the worship of that god at Delphi, and with the music of the cithara. The theme of a musical contest between man and god is found in the legend of Marsyas (cf. XVII n. 20).

21. Euterpe, the muse of music.

22. Evoe or Evohe, the Bacchanalian cry.

XXXII

1. Jean Moréas (Iannis Papadiamantopoulos, 1856-1910), Greek-born French poet and prose writer, came to Paris in the mid-1870s. He wrote two volumes of Symbolist verse, but later founded the École Romane, calling for a return to classic forms.

2. Chlamys, a short mantle worn by men in ancient Greece.

3. Pierre Alexis, vicomte de Ponson du Terrail (1829-71), French popular and prolific novelist.

4. Vsevolod Krestovsky (1840-95), poet and novelist.

5. Vladislav Khodasevich (1886-1939), regarded by some as one of the greatest Russian poets of the century. He wrote his best verse after emigrating to Paris in 1922, where he became a central figure in emigré literary circles.

6. Fyodor Tyutchev (1803-73), lyric poet. His small body of works consists of about 400 poems, which rarely run more than 20 lines.

Similarly, Innokenty Annensky (1856-1909) published only two collections of verse—*Quiet Songs* (1904) and *The Cypress Chest* (1910). The latter is reviewed in XIV.

7. Alexei Tolstoi (1883-1945), poet, playwright and journalist. He published two collections of verse before the Revolution: *Lyrics* (1907), and *Beyond the Blue Rivers* (1911), but he is best known for his historical novels, including the trilogy *The Road to Calvary* (1918-23) which earned him the Stalin Prize in 1942.

8. François Vielé-Griffin (1863-1937), American-born French poet, associated with the Symbolists. A master of vers libre, he wrote of the beauties of Touraine in a number of early collections. His later works reflect his interest in Hellenic and Medieval Germanic legend.

9. The first lines of the opening poem of Ivanov's first collection *Pilot Stars* (1903).

10. The first lines of the poem "Elisaveta" from *Ascent* (*Voskhozhdenie*, 1913).

11. From a lyric by Kuzmin.

12. The article to which Gumilev refers is "Lettres russes. Les Poètes. Futurisme, Akméisme, Adamisme, etc." (*Mercure de France*, 1 November 1913, pp. 201-204).

XXXIII

1. Maria Evgenevna Levberg (1894-1934), poet and translator; published no other collections of verse.

2. Leonid Lvovich Berman also published *New Troy* (*Novaia Troia*, 1921).

3. Phoebus, one of the epithets for Apollo.

4. The Russian *tumba* is used jocularly to refer to a clumsy, fat person, much as post can by used as a type of lifelessness, stupidity or ignorance.

5. Alexander ("Sandro") Akimovich Korona (?-1967), published no other collections. He emigrated after the Revolution to Italy, France and finally the USA.

6. From a Tatar song in Pushkin's *The Fountain of Bakhchisarai* (1822), 11. 131-34.

7. Pierre Louÿs (1870-1925) French novelist and poet of the Parnassian school, classical scholar.

8. *Alexandrian Songs* appeared first in the July, 1907 issue of *Scales*. The complete series was included in Kuzmin's first book of verse, *Nets* (1908), and issued in a separate collection only in 1921. English translation in M. Kuzmin, *Wings: Prose and*

Poetry (Ann Arbor, 1972).

9. Chrolli (pseudonym of Konstantin Fastovich Tarasov) published a second collection, *Son of Faust* (1916).

10. Tikhon Churilin (c. 1890-1944). His second collection was published in 1918. In 1940 a small book of his poems appeared in Moscow.

11. Prince G. Gagarin. This was his last published work. For Gumilev's uncharitable comments on Daniil Ratgauz, to whom he is compared, see XII.

12. Count Alexander A. Saltykov, publicist in Germany after the Revolution. This is his only collection of poems.

13. This passage contains the shards of Saltykov's considerable classical learning: *Sospita* (savior) is a standard epithet for Juno, while *Populona* (from *populo*—to ravage, destroy) is not. *Iuturna,* a nymph, sister of Turnus, King of the Rutuli, and originally a goddess of a spring near Lavinium, was later associated with a fountain in the Forum of Rome, where the Temple of Janus stood, etc., etc.

14. Leonid Andreev (1871-1919), short-story writer and playwright. "In the Fog" deals with a student who contracts syphilis, kills the prostitute who infected him and then commits suicide.

15. Vladimir Prussak. His second collection was published in Irkutsk in 1917.

XXXIV

1. Georgy Adamovich (b. 1894), minor poet associated with the Acmeists. He published other collections of verse, including *Purgatory* (1922) and *In the West* (Paris, 1939).

2. Shemakha, ancient city in Azerbaijan, important in the silk trade in the sixteenth century, destroyed by earthquake in 1902.

3. "Ballad" was published in *The Cypress Chest* (1910) under "Funereal Triptych," p. 31.

4. Georgy Ivanov's first collection *Chamber* (1914), is reviewed in XXXII.

5. *Capital and Country-seat*—a Russian version of *Town and Country*.

6. Mikhail Lozinsky (1886-1955), minor poet associated with the Acmeists, and voluminous translator of Dante, Moliere, Corneille, Shakespeare. His single collection of poems, *Mountain Spring*, appeared in two editions (1916, 1922).

7. Principal characters in Byron's Faustian tragedy *Manfred* (1817) and his dramatic poem *Cain, a Mystery* (1821).

8. Balmont's "Dead Ships" appeared in the cycle *Silence* (*Tishina*, 1898).

9. *Stone.* SPb: Akmè, 1913. 34 pages. 2nd edition, Petrograd: Giperborei, 1916. 91 pages.

XXXV

1. Mikhail Struve (1890-1948), member of the Acmeist circle Guild of Poets, and friend of Gumilev. He emigrated to Paris.

XXXVI

1. I was unable to find any record of other books by Konstantin Lyandau.

XXXVII

1. The obituaries appeared under separate title immediately after Gumilev's regular "Letter on Russian Poetry" (XIX in this volume).

2. Compare the critic's evaluation of Fofanov's work here with the much less complimentary review in XI.

3. Longfellow's poem "Day is Done" (Fall, 1844),printed as the proem to *The Waif* (1844). The passage reads:

> ... *The bards sublime,*
> *Whose distant footsteps echo*
> *Through the corridors of Time.*

XXXVIII

1. Printed as the foreword to the first volume of A.K. Tolstoi's *Selected Works* (Berlin-Petrograd-Moscow: Grezhbin, 1923), edited by Gumilev. Only the first volume was completed.

2. Alexei Zhemchuzhnikov (1821-1908) and his brother Vladimir (1830-84). In addition to collaborating with A.K. Tolstoi, Alexei Zhemchuzhnikov also wrote some civic poetry at the turn of the century.

XXXIX

1. Kornei Chukovsky (1892-1969), literary critic, writer of children's books, translator. Before the Revolution, he was very active in avant-garde literary circles.

2. Tarbagatai, mountain range in Central Asia, on the border of Kazakhstan and Sinkiang Province.

XL

1. Balmont's numerous translations include: Shelley's closet drama *Prometheus Unbound* (1820)—issued in SPb.: Znanie, 1904. The collected works of Calderon, Moscow, 1900-12. 3 vols. *Shakuntala*, a play by the fifth century Indian poet and dramatist Kalidasa. M. and S.: Sabashnikov, 1915. The Georgian epic *Bearer of the Snow-Leopard Skin*. Moscow, 1917.